Museums and Galleries

Museums and Galleries

A Window into History

Rafeal Mechlore

WSM Publisher

CONTENTS

INDEX 1

INTRODUCTION 3

Chapter 1   18

Chapter 2   34

Chapter 3   56

Chapter 4   74

Chapter 5   93

Chapter 6   108

Chapter 7   129

Chapter 8   150

Chapter 9   164

INDEX

Introduction

1. The significance of museums and galleries in preserving history
2. The role of museums in educating, inspiring, and connecting people to the past
3. Overview of the book's structure and main themes

Chapter 1: The Evolution of Museums
1.1 The origins of museums and galleries
1.2 Historical development and the changing purpose of museums
1.3 Key figures and milestones in the history of museums
1.4 The impact of technology on modern museums

Chapter 2: Types of Museums and Galleries
2.1 Art museums and galleries
2.2 Natural history museums
2.3 Science and technology museums
2.4 History and cultural heritage museums
2.5 Specialized and unique museums
2.6 Virtual museums and the digital era

Chapter 3: Curating and Conservation
3.1 The role of curators in shaping museum collections
3.2 Conservation and preservation of artifacts
3.3 Ethical dilemmas in museum curation

Chapter 4: Museums as Educational Institutions
4.1 The educational mission of museums
4.2 Educational programs and initiatives
4.3 Museums and formal education

4.4 The role of museums in promoting lifelong learning

Chapter 5: Museums and Cultural Heritage
5.1 The preservation of cultural heritage in museums
5.2 The repatriation debate
5.3 Museums and cultural diplomacy

Chapter 6: Museums and Community Engagement
6.1 Museums as community hubs
6.2 Outreach programs and initiatives
6.3 Collaborations with local communities

Chapter 7: Technological Advancements in Museums
7.1 Virtual reality and augmented reality in museums
7.2 Interactive exhibits and digital storytelling
7.3 Online collections and virtual tours
7.4 Challenges and opportunities of technology in museums

Chapter 8: Museums in a Global Context
8.1 International cooperation in the museum world
8.2 The role of museums in fostering cross-cultural understanding

Chapter 9: The Future of Museums
9.1 Emerging trends and challenges
9.2 Sustainability and environmental responsibility in museums
9.3 Museums and social justice
9.4 Speculations on the future of museums

INTRODUCTION

It would be an oversimplification to claim that museums and galleries are only storage facilities for relics or works of art; they house much more than that. They are, in point of fact, potent gates to the past, conserving the core of human history, culture, and innovation in the process. The moment you enter these sacred chambers, it is as if you are setting off on an epic adventure through time. Here, the histories of civilizations, societies, and individuals have been painstakingly collected and displayed in such a way that they call us to decipher the mysteries of our collective human tale. The documentary titled "Museums and Galleries: A Window into History" is an examination of the enormous significance of these cultural institutions and the role that they play in radically reshaping our perception of the wider world.

Museums have developed over the course of history, transcending their original function as the private collections of wealthy individuals to become public gathering places for a wider audience. The fact that they came into existence is evidence that people have always had a strong desire to protect, understand, and disseminate our diverse history. From their more humble beginnings as cabinets of curiosities and early Wunderkammers, through the establishment of public museums during the Enlightenment, and on into the subsequent diversification into specialized institutions, museums have come to occupy a central place in the preservation and dissemination of human knowledge. This book strives to follow this progression by providing light on the significant people, historical landmarks, and societal upheavals that have influenced the present museum scene. The book also aims to provide an overview of the history of museum architecture.

The landscape of museums and galleries is a rich tapestry of diversity, embracing a wide variety of art forms and academic fields. There are the magnificent art museums and galleries that serve as havens for human creativity and expression by providing a home for the works of renowned painters and storing the masterpieces created by those artists. Natural history museums include a staggering variety of specimens that demonstrate the wonders of our planet's flora and wildlife. These museums serve as living testimonies to the natural world's myriad of wondrous phenomena, and they house a collection that is truly stunning. The flames of curiosity and creativity are fanned by science and technology museums, which also showcase the incredible progress that has been made by human ingenuity throughout the years. Museums of history and cultural heritage play the role of storytellers by crafting narratives about societies that no longer exist and displaying the tangible relics of those societies' existence. Unique and specialized museums cater to a wide variety of specific interests, ranging from offbeat topics to certain historical eras, and provide visitors with a more individualized and in-depth experience as a result. Virtual museums have developed as an innovative form of accessing and experiencing history with the dawn of the digital era. These museums bring the wonders of the past directly to our fingertips, making history more accessible than ever before. This book makes an effort to shed light on these various dimensions, illuminating the multidimensional nature of museums and galleries as the stewards of our shared cultural legacy.

The duties of curation and conservation play an essential part in the operation of museums. Museums are not only locations for the warehousing of items; rather, they are living organisms that require the skills of qualified curators in order to build narratives and generate meaningful experiences for visitors. It is only through the painstaking process of conservation and preservation that these priceless relics are able to endure the ravages of time and continue to provide future generations with the opportunity to learn about the past. This book examines the complex obligations of curators, delving into their creative processes as well as the difficulties and ethical conundrums they face in the process of curating collections. It also sheds focus on the important work that conservationists do, highlighting the efforts they make to preserve artifacts for future generations and to restore them when they become damaged. This book emphasizes the critical role that curation and conservation play in maintaining the authenticity of museum collections by examining a variety of case studies and looking at them through the same lens.

The experience of visiting a museum should always center on learning. These establishments act as crucial hubs for learning by providing visitors of all ages with immersive programs, interactive exhibitions, and educational initiatives that are geared toward the institution's particular subject matter. Visits to museums are frequently used as an extension of classroom learning in schools. This provides students with the opportunity to engage with history, art, and science in a manner that is both physical and immersive. In addition, museums encourage lifelong learning by providing a venue in which visitors can broaden their horizons intellectually and develop a more in-depth comprehension of the world in which they live. This book sheds light on the educational role that museums play in society by highlighting their potential to stimulate visitors' inquisitiveness, critical thinking, and creative abilities. This article investigates the numerous educational programs and initiatives that are provided by museums, highlighting the essential role that museums play in sculpting the intellectual and cultural landscape of society.

The preservation of cultural history is the primary focus of museums and art galleries. These institutions are the bulwarks of tradition, memory, and collective identity; as such, they play an important part in the preservation of both the tangible and intangible components of cultural identity. They have been assigned with the mission of preserving for future generations cultural treasures, historical tales, and artworks. However, the topic of cultural heritage preservation is not without its complexity, as museums struggle with questions of provenance, ownership, and the ethical repatriation of items to the nations in which they were first discovered. This book goes deep into the complex conversation that surrounds the preservation of cultural heritage. It sheds light on the difficulties and opportunities that museums face in their efforts to maintain and promote cultural variety.

In addition to this, it investigates the part that museums play in cultural diplomacy, focusing on their ability to promote cross-cultural communication and comprehension on a worldwide scale.

Museums are not independent institutions; rather, they are dynamic venues that survive through the engagement of the local community and partnership with other organizations. They act as centers of cultural activity, assisting in the development of linkages and interactions with the communities in the surrounding area and encouraging active involvement in the programs and projects being offered. By bridging the gap between museums and the general public through the use of outreach programs, community events, and joint initiatives, museums are able to cultivate a sense of ownership and inclusivity. This book explores the transformative power of community engagement and demonstrates how museums have become essential components of local communities, generating social change and empowering local residents through their outreach initiatives. It shows the symbiotic link between museums and the communities that surround them via captivating case studies, putting an emphasis on the crucial role that community engagement plays in the protection and development of cultural heritage.

In this day and age, which is characterized by the rapid growth of technology, museums have embraced innovation in order to improve the experience of their visitors and extend their reach. The way that museums display and understand history has been altered by technologies such as virtual reality, augmented reality, interactive exhibitions, and digital storytelling. These technologies make it possible for visitors to enjoy experiences that are immersive, engaging, and transcendent of their physical limits. The accessibility of the world's cultural assets to an audience from all over the world has been made possible by the proliferation of online collections and virtual tours. This has helped people develop a greater appreciation for the richness of human legacy and has transcended geographical boundaries. This book investigates the interface of technology and museums and aims to shed light on the transformative potential of digital innovations in boosting the accessibility and impact of museum experiences. In addition to this, it discusses the potential and difficulties that are given by technological advancements, and it encourages museums to find a middle ground between traditional preservation methods and innovative digital efforts.

The functioning of museums takes place within a global setting, which helps to encourage international cooperation and a knowledge of other cultures. They play an important role as platforms for cultural exchange, which helps to facilitate communication and cooperation between different communities and nations. Museums encourage a deeper awareness of other cultures, histories, and traditions by means of the exhibitions, events, and initiatives they host. This helps to create empathy and respect for the diverse peoples and civilizations that inhabit the world. This book examines museums from a global perspective, focusing on the essential role they play in promoting intercultural understanding and cultivating a sense of global citizenship. It does so by presenting case studies of museums that have made major contributions to international cultural diplomacy.

These museums are highlighted because of the impact they have had on developing mutual respect and admiration across various cultures and nations.

As museums attempt to make sense of the complexities of the modern day, they are confronted with a wide variety of obstacles and opportunities that will influence their path into the future. Museums face both challenges and opportunities in maintaining their relevance and resiliency as a result of emerging trends, technological breakthroughs, concerns about environmental sustainability, and the changing cultural landscape. This book takes a look into the distant future to speculate on the future of museums and galleries, as well as the various pathways by which these establishments can adapt to and survive in a world that is changing at an accelerated rate. It calls for a renewed commitment to the protection and promotion of cultural legacy for future generations, highlighting the essential role that museums play in campaigning for environmental stewardship and social justice.

1. **The significance of museums and galleries in preserving history**
   Museums and art galleries are venerated as holy places because of the vital role they play in conserving and exhibiting historical artifacts and information. These cultural sanctuaries play an essential part in preserving the collective memory of humanity. They make certain that the tales, objects, and legacies of our past are not obliterated by the sands of time by ensuring that they are kept safe. They are windows into history, providing a palpable and immersive experience that helps us to connect with our heritage, learn from our predecessors, and get a deeper respect for the nuances of our collective past. Their relevance extends far beyond the simple act of collecting artifacts; instead, they are windows into history.

Museums are charged with the responsibility of safeguarding our cultural, artistic, and scientific history. They are stores of valuables that span the entirety of human history, storing anything from ancient antiquities to modern works of art. These establishments are known as treasury repositories. These institutions take measures to safeguard the material relics of our history from the ravages of time, hazards posed by the natural world, and the indifference of modern society. It is possible to look at the role that museums play in the maintenance of history from a variety of perspectives, and each one will shed light on a different feature of their enduring significance.

Museums play an important role in the preservation of our cultural legacy and are often referred to as "guardians." They preserve the items, records, artworks, and historical relics that are physical manifestations of human civilization and are housed within the institutions. These objects may take the form of sculptures, paintings, pottery, textiles, manuscripts, and a variety of other types of artwork. Museums assure the long-term preservation of these things by providing them with painstaking care and attention.

This preservation extends not just to the physical protection of items but also to the conservation of the narratives, traditions, and practices that are embedded within them. These cultural treasures are preserved in museums, giving future generations the opportunity to connect with their ancestors and gain an understanding of the complex web that is human history.

Documentation of the Past: Museums play an essential role as important archives for the preservation of historical documentation. They amass, classify, and make available an extensive variety of primary source documents, such as letters, diaries, pictures, and government records. Documents such as this are essential for researchers, historians, and other academics who are attempting to decipher the complexity of the past. The painstaking preservation of such items at museums contributes to the authenticity and depth of historical narratives, revealing light on the lives of individuals, the dynamics of communities, and the development of cultural traditions.

Legacy of Art: The preservation of humanity's artistic legacy relies heavily on art institutions such as museums and galleries, in particular. They store works of art that span several centuries, from the greatest masterpieces of the past to the most recent creations of artists living and working now. The preservation efforts of these institutions help to ensure that the artistic expressions of painters, sculptors, and other artists are not destroyed, stolen, or neglected. Museums provide a visual record of the developing styles, techniques, and topics that have distinguished the world of art by preserving the works that are on display in their collections.

Specimens of Scientific Interest Natural history museums play an important role in the conservation of scientific specimens. These institutions are responsible for the care and preservation of a diverse array of fossils, taxidermy animals, mineral collections, and other biological, geological, and paleontological objects. For the purposes of scientific investigation, specimens of this kind are essential because they provide information about the biodiversity, evolution, and geological history of the natural world. The significance of natural history museums in preserving history extends to our comprehension of the ecological history of the planet as well as the relevance of that history to modern environmental concerns.

Artifacts of Culture: Cultural history museums house a wide variety of artifacts, such as tools, clothes, household items, and religious relics. These artifacts offer insights into the daily lives and belief systems of societies of the past and may be found in museums all over the world. These artifacts are like windows into the past because they provide a direct link to the individuals who formerly made use of them. Museums make it possible for visitors to experience the customs and rituals of bygone eras by preserving and displaying the things that were used in those times.

Discoveries in the Field of Archaeology The archiving and storage of archaeological finds is mostly the responsibility of museums. Archaeologists search for and excavate ancient cities, burial grounds, and artifacts in order to give light on civilizations that have been extinct for a very long time. These discoveries are frequently delicate and prone to degeneration after they have been subjected to the external conditions. The archaeological finds are preserved, maintained, and made available to the public by museums. Museums also play an important role in education. Museums contribute to our understanding of ancient cultures and the role they played in the development of human history through the exhibition and research of their collections.

The generational divide can be bridged through museums because they provide visitors of all ages with the opportunity to engage with and learn from the past. They offer a place where adults of all generations, including parents and grandparents, as well as children, may learn about history together. The immersive experiences provided by museums appeal to a variety of learning methods and make history approachable and interesting for people of all ages. Museums encourage a sense of continuity and an understanding that is shared among multiple generations by collecting, preserving, and compellingly presenting historical information.

Museums aren't only places to store artifacts; they're also archives for the stories and narratives associated with those objects. They are responsible for the curation of exhibitions that tell the tales of people, communities, and significant events in history. These tales, which can be about the challenges of a minority population, the life of a famous artist, or the history of an old civilization, are the ones that museums work to preserve and share with others.

They create a space for empathetic understanding, introspection, and a more profound appreciation of the human experience as a result of their actions. Museums have made a commitment to representing a wide variety of viewpoints and experiences as part of their mission to be inclusive and diverse. They hope to be inclusive venues that highlight the history and accomplishments of underrepresented communities, thereby challenging standard historical narratives that may have left out certain voices or distorted others. Museums contribute to a more just and complete understanding of our common history by recognizing and conserving the histories of a wide variety of cultures and communities.

Research and Academic Study: Researchers and academics working in a wide variety of disciplines find museums to be indispensable resources. They make primary source materials, artworks, specimens, and historical data available to the public. In-depth studies, the generation of new information, and contributions to the academic discourse are all possible outcomes of researchers delving into the collections of museums. Museums contribute to the continuing investigation and reassessment of history by providing spaces like this one. Museums are essential to the formation and maintenance of cultural identities, and play a vital part in this process. They give communities places to celebrate their cultural history and the traditions they have upheld for generations. Museums preserve objects and works of art that serve as physical symbols of cultural identity. This helps members of the community feel a feeling of pride and a sense of continuity in their lives. Museums make an important contribution to the maintenance of cultural diversity in a world that is always evolving through their preservation of various aspects of culture.

Instruments of Learning: Today's museums have evolved into dynamic educational organizations. They provide a wide variety of educational opportunities, including programs, workshops, and exhibitions, with the goal of attracting students of all ages. An interactive and experiential method of learning about history, art, and science is available to educational groups, students, and people who are learning throughout their lives. As a result of their ability to foster creative and analytical thinking, curiosity, and a profound respect for knowledge, museums are extremely useful teaching instruments.

Encouragement of Critical Thinking: Museums should encourage visitors to engage with the exhibits they view and to think critically about what they see. Visitors are urged to actively participate in the conversation by actively participating in the conversation by asking questions, forming their own ideas, and engaging in intellectual dialogue rather than passively ingesting information. This not only helps visitors gain a more in-depth comprehension of historical events, but it also pushes them to challenge previously held beliefs and investigate alternative points of view.

Museums are in a unique position to play a role in the promotion of cultural interchange on a national and even international scale. They organize exhibitions that highlight the art, history, and culture of a variety of countries around the world. These displays act as windows into different societies, so creating an awareness and understanding of each other's cultures. Museums contribute to diplomacy, peace, and a more interconnected globe by providing an environment that encourages cultural interaction.

Engagement with the Public and Connection to the Community Museums are not solitary institutions but rather thriving locations that relate to the community. They inspire feelings of awe and curiosity, as well as a sense of connection to the past. Museums attract visitors from all walks of life who are interested in discovering their origins, gaining knowledge about other cultures, and engaging with the narratives and artifacts that have shaped our collective history.

Interdisciplinary Methodology: When teaching about the past, museums frequently adopt an interdisciplinary methodology.

They give a comprehensive perspective of the past by combining aspects of art, science, history, and culture into a single narrative. This method is extremely helpful in tearing down the traditional walls that separate different areas of knowledge and encouraging a more holistic comprehension of the complexity of history.

Inspiration for Creativity: Artists, Writers, Filmmakers, and Creators of All Kinds Can Find Inspiration at Museums Museums serve as sources of inspiration for creators of all kinds. Many times, fresh ideas, creative works, and novel ways of thinking are sparked by the rich tapestry of history and art that is on exhibit within their walls. Individuals are encouraged to reinterpret the past in ways that are modern and inventive when they visit museums, which is a source of creativity that museums supply.

A Platform for Contemplation: Museums provide visitors with a serene and reflective environment in which they can think about the world's history. Museums create an environment that is conducive to introspection, deliberation, and the exploration of complicated ideas and feelings. This can be accomplished in a variety of ways, including the tranquility of an art gallery or the immersive experience of a historical display.

Museums offer a physical anchor for the preservation of historical documents, artworks, and artifacts in an age when information can be fleeting and easily lost due to the prevalence of digital technology. This allows museums to combat the ephemeral nature of digital information. The fact that museum collections are held in tangible form ensures that they will continue to be accessible and relevant even as digital formats continue to develop and adapt. Avoiding the Erosion of Cultural Memory If it weren't for museums, the collective cultural memory of our society would be in danger of disintegrating.

It would be easy for things like tales, objects, and traditions to fall into disrepair, destruction, or neglect. The nation's museums serve as strongholds against this erosion of our cultural heritage, ensuring that it is preserved in its full vitality while still remaining easily accessible and widely cherished.

2. **The role of museums in educating, inspiring, and connecting people to the past**

    Museums are not only static storage facilities for relics and works of art; rather, they have evolved into active educational institutions that play an important and diversified role in the community. They serve as important hubs for learning, wellsprings of creativity, and potent conduits that link modern people to their ancestors and the past. Museums have the ability to educate, inspire, and make relationships by providing visitors of various ages, backgrounds, and interests with a variety of experiences that are both immersive and interactive. In this paper, we will delve into the tremendous relevance of museums as educational institutions, studying their role in stimulating innovation and promoting a deeper understanding of the past. This topic will be covered in further depth later in the paper.

    The Role of Museums as Educational Establishments

    Education in an Official Capsule Museums are frequently used as adjuncts in the official education system. They are visited by students from local schools, colleges, and universities on educational excursions, which helps students supplement the knowledge they gain in the classroom with experiences from the real world. Students' knowledge of subjects like history, art, science, and culture can be significantly improved through the combination of traditional schooling with trips to museums.

    Programs That Are Based On A Curriculum Many museums offer educational programs that are based on a curriculum and are designed to coincide with school curricula. These programs provide educators a variety of tools and activities designed to bridge the gap between what their students learn in the classroom and what they see in the museum, so fostering a more profound comprehension of the material.

    Learning Through Doing: Hands-On Learning is encouraged in museums through the use of interactive displays and activities. Visitors are invited to touch artifacts and items, experiment with them, and engage with them, all of which develop a deeper connection with the information being presented. Experiments that allow visitors to participate and get a better understanding of scientific principles through direct experience are frequently found in science museums, for instance.

    Experiences That Engage various Senses The purpose of museums is to enhance the learning process by providing visitors with opportunities to engage various senses. Visitors may be able to experience a historical period through a variety of senses, including hearing the sounds of the time period, seeing vivid depictions of artwork, smelling the aromas of old societies, and even tasting cuisines from various countries. These encounters engage multiple senses, which contribute to the formation of enduring impressions and the facilitation of a more profound grasp of the material.

Lifelong Learning Museums are not limited to only providing a formal education; rather, they also serve to those who are interested in learning throughout their lives. Adults of all ages, including elders, can participate in intellectually enriching activities like seminars, talks, and other events. The concept that education should continue throughout one's life is bolstered by museums, which also make available additional learning opportunities for adults who have completed their formal schooling.

Education in the Digital Age: As we have moved into the digital age, educational institutions such as museums have embraced technology as a teaching tool. They make their instructional content available online in the form of resources, virtual tours, and digital collections, so that it can be accessed by people all over the world. Through the use of digital outreach, they are able to reach more people and ensure that education is not limited to a specific location.

Education for People of All Ages Museums are designed to accommodate visitors of all ages, from young children to elderly people. They ensure that the educational opportunities they provide are accessible to people of all ages by providing information and experiences that are suitable for that specific ages. Play and exploration are two of the primary activities encouraged at children's museums, which are intended to stimulate and educate young visitors.

Motivating Creative Thinking

Exposure to Art and Culture: Visitors to art museums and galleries are presented with a diverse array of artistic styles, ranging from the traditional to the cutting edge. They invite audiences to look at the world in novel and inventive ways through the use of paintings, sculptures, and installations in their exhibitions. Being exposed to a variety of artistic expressions is proven to boost creative thought.

Inspiration from Across the Disciplines: Many museums successfully combine aspects of art, science, history, and culture in their exhibits. This method of approaching problems from a variety of perspectives allows individuals to think creatively and draw connections between concepts from a range of disciplines. For example, an art museum might organize shows that investigate the ways in which art and science cross with one another.

Exhibits That Are Interactive Many museums have exhibits that are interactive and invite visitors to participate in a variety of creative activities. Experiments that visitors can try their hands at at science museums, for instance, are designed to pique their attention and encourage them to become curious about the world around them. Visitors are encouraged to become active participants in the creative process through the use of these activities.

Exploration of Cultural Heritage Museums that concentrate on cultural history and heritage are
excellent resources for learning about the various traditions, practices, and stories that are associated with a variety of groups. This investigation of cultural diversity can motivate individuals to cherish their own heritage while also learning about the heritage of others and can also develop an appreciation for the richness of human expression.

Modern Topics Explored in Museums Some museums explore modern topics such as social justice, climate change, and identity through the use of dialogues. These exhibitions and events have the potential to ignite vital conversations and motivate individuals to engage with current concerns creatively, whether it be through the creation of art, participation in activist movements, or the development of novel solutions.

Museums frequently serve as sites for artistic expression, as they hold art exhibitions, performances, and other activities. These museums provide spaces for artistic expression. They make it possible for artists to share their work with others and serve as a source of creative motivation for those around them.

Bringing People Closer to Their History

Museums frequently utilize narrative exhibition design, which involves the utilization of storytelling techniques in order to completely immerse visitors in the historical events and circumstances being presented. By taking this technique, visitors are given the opportunity to put themselves in the position of people who lived in the past and gain an understanding of the world from their point of view.

Historical objects are Protected and Preserved Museums take great care to protect historical objects and ensure that they will continue to be available to visitors for many decades to come. Visitors are able to get a close-up look at these artifacts, creating a direct and palpable link between themselves and the people and events that occurred in the past.

Contextual interpretation is something that museums offer to their visitors in order to assist them in comprehending the importance of the items and pieces of art on display. They provide an explanation of the historical, cultural, and social circumstances in which these things were created, so boosting visitors' understanding of history and their connection to it.

Archaeological Discoveries and Anthropological Artifacts: It's not uncommon for museums to house archaeological discoveries and anthropological artifacts, both of which can provide light on ancient civilizations and the evolution of humans. These displays enable visitors to investigate the ways of life and cultures of our ancestors, so bridging the gap between the present and the distant past.

Museums give visitors the opportunity to examine their personal histories as well as the histories of their communities and society as a whole through various programs and exhibits.

Museums sometimes encourage visitors to engage with their own personal histories as well as the histories of their communities through activities such as genealogical research, oral history projects, and displays that highlight local heritage.

The opportunity to reflect on the lessons that history has taught us can be found in the settings that museums provide. Visitors are encouraged to reflect on the legacy of bygone deeds and behaviors, the significance of bygone occurrences, and the bearing of history on the problems of the present day. Individuals are able to gain wisdom from their experiences and make better choices in the present as a result of these thoughts.

Emotional ties: Museums frequently forge emotional ties between visitors and the past via the cultivation of empathy and the exchange of similar experiences. Museums dedicated to the Holocaust, for instance, are known to elicit strong feelings, prompting visitors to contemplate the atrocities of the past and encourage them to work toward creating a more compassionate and just society. Museums play a significant role in the promotion of cultural identity by conserving and celebrating the history and heritage of a variety of groups. This enables the museums to play a role in the promotion of cultural identity. This helps to cultivate a sense of belonging and connection among the people of the community and gives them the opportunity to perceive themselves as a part of a more comprehensive historical story.

Reenactments and Living History: Some museums conduct reenactments and living history events that allow visitors to walk into the past and experience what it was like to live during that time. Individuals are given the opportunity to become active participants in history through the medium of these interactive experiences, which create a concrete connection to historical eras and events.

Understanding on a Global and Cross-Cultural Scale: Global and cross-cultural topics are frequently investigated in museums. They provide an overview of the history and culture of various areas, leading to a greater comprehension and respect of the variety of human communities. This comprehension helps people feel more connected to the wider world and motivates them to adopt a worldview that is more inclusive.

3. **Overview of the book's structure and main themes**

This book, titled "Museums and Galleries: A Window into History," is an in-depth investigation into the significant role that museums and galleries play in the maintenance and display of historical artifacts, as well as cultural and artistic works. The reader will find a rich tapestry of subjects and themes that delve into the many facets that play a role in the role that these cultural organizations play inside its pages. This summary will provide insight into the structure of the book as well as the primary issues that it examines, and it will serve as a road map for the intellectual adventure that lies ahead.

Format of the Book

The path that the reader will take through the world of museums and galleries is laid out in a logical and systematic manner for them to follow in this book. Each subsequent part has been thoughtfully constructed to expand upon the last one, eventually elucidating the role that these organizations play in conserving and disseminating historical knowledge.

The book starts off with a detailed introduction that lays the groundwork for the subsequent explorations that are going to take place. It presents the idea of museums as "windows into history" and highlights the vital role that museums play in our comprehension of the past. The introduction provides a summary of the organization of the book and gives a preview of the topics that will be discussed in the succeeding chapters.

The First Chapter: The Development of Museums: This chapter will take readers on a journey through history, chronicling the development of museums from their early beginnings as private collections and cabinets of curiosity to the complex and diverse institutions that we know today. It focuses on the influential people and significant events that have had a role in the evolution of museums.

Chapter 2: The Wide-Ranging Collections of Museums: This chapter examines the different types of museums, including art museums and galleries, natural history museums, science and technology museums, history museums, and specialty or unusual museums. The discussion is based on the historical framework presented in the previous chapter. It examines the distinctive qualities and responsibilities of each variety, putting an emphasis on the differences among them.

Museums are not simply static storage areas; rather, they are dynamic locations that call for knowledgeable curation and conservation efforts. This topic will be covered in Chapter 3. This chapter examines the responsibilities of curators as well as the difficulties associated with the process of maintaining and conserving priceless items.

In addition to this, it discusses moral conundrums that are associated with repatriation and gives case examples of conservation and preservation initiatives that are particularly noteworthy.

Education and Continuous Education Museums play an essential role in the educational process. This chapter sheds light on their educational objective and investigates the varied activities that they provide, which range from visits to schools to public talks. It highlights the significant role that museums play in formal education as well as in the promotion of learning that continues throughout one's life by offering experiences that are enriching to visitors of all ages.

Museums play an important role in the process of maintaining cultural heritage and in the promotion of international cultural diplomacy (Chapter 5: Cultural Heritage and Diplomacy). This chapter investigates the issues that surround the repatriation of artifacts and the wider ramifications that this topic has for the community of museums located all over the world. Additionally, case examples of museums that are firmly ingrained in their local communities and that generate global links are presented.

Technology is having a profound effect on museums in this age of digitalization, and this chapter focuses on the intersection of technology and innovation. This chapter investigates the role that augmented reality, virtual reality, interactive exhibits, and digital storytelling have in the overall experience that a tourist has at an attraction. In addition to this, it investigates the potential and difficulties that new technology presents to museums.

The book takes a look at international cooperation, cultural exchange, and cross-cultural understanding via the lens of museums in Chapter 7 of the book, which is titled "Global Perspective." It sheds light on the essential part that museums play in the process of building relationships between people all over the world.

The Future of Museums is Discussed in Chapter 8. In the final chapter, we take a look into the future of museums and speculate on the role they will play in environmental responsibility, social justice, and the ever-changing cultural landscape. It discusses new tendencies, difficulties, and opportunities, and it provides insights into what the future holds for these cultural organizations.

In its last chapter, the author provides a concise summary of the most important insights and emphasizes the enduring value of museums as windows into history. This underscores their important role in preserving and presenting history, as well as their power to inspire, educate, and link people to their cultural heritage.

Principal Concepts

Museums play an important role in the preservation of cultural heritage by ensuring that objects, works of art, and historical narratives are accessible to future generations. This theme places an emphasis on the critical function that museums fulfill in the preservation of both the material and immaterial facets of human culture.

Educational Purpose: Museums play an important role in society as dynamic educational organizations that inspire a passion for both learning and discovery. They offer both formal and informal education, making it possible for people of varying ages and socioeconomic backgrounds to get access to knowledge.

Expertise in Curatorial Matters and Conservation: The focus of this theme is on the significance of expertise in curatorial matters and conservation in the upkeep of the integrity of museum collections. It explores the creative processes that curators go through as well as the difficulties that come with maintaining such items.

Motivating People to Think Creatively Museums motivate visitors to think creatively by presenting them with a wide variety of artistic expressions and encouraging inventive thought. They provide outlets for creative expression and open doors for individuals to interact with the wider world in imaginative ways.

Connection to the Past: Museums are able to build connections between the present and the past, which enables visitors to get a more in-depth comprehension of historical events. In order to create a connection between people and the past, they provide narrative display design, the preservation of historical items, and emotional engagement.

Museums work hard to represent a wide variety of peoples' points of view and experiences through inclusive programming. The celebration of cultural variety and the questioning of established historical narratives both contribute to the development of an understanding that is more egalitarian and comprehensive of our collective history.

Museums foster intercultural understanding and act as platforms for the interaction of different cultures from around the world. This contributes to global perspective and cultural diplomacy. They encourage conversation, collaboration, and mutual respect among different cultures and nations all around the world.

Technology & Innovation: This theme investigates the ways in which museums are adjusting to the digital age by utilizing technology to improve the experience of museum visitors. In addition to this, it discusses the potential and difficulties posed by technological advancements.

The book speculates on the future of museums, taking into consideration their role in environmental responsibility, social justice, and a developing cultural landscape. The title of the book comes from the chapter titled "The Future of Museums." It sheds light on developing tendencies and inspires museums to evolve in order to survive and thrive in a dynamic world.

Chapter 1

The Evolution of Museums

Over the course of history, there has been a considerable shift toward the development of museums, which have shifted from being exclusive private collections to openly accessible public institutions that appeal to a variety of audiences. The long and illustrious history of museums is evidence that people have always been fascinated with the idea of preserving and providing explanations for the cultural, artistic, and scientific artifacts of the world. The development of museums can be broken down into a number of distinct periods, each of which can be identified by unique alterations in collection techniques, curatorial approaches, and the general public's opinion of these cultural institutions. This in-depth look at the history of museums throws light on the significant landmarks, prominent figures, and societal shifts that have contributed to the formation of the museum landscape as we know it today.

The Beginnings: Objects Kept in Display Cases

Cabinets of Curiosity and Wunderkammers are two examples of the forerunners to modern

museums that can be traced all the way back to the Renaissance period in Europe, which is when the concept of museums as we know them today first developed. These were private collections that were often owned by wealthy individuals, members of the nobility, or academics who were attracted by the wonders of the natural world, rare objects, and the artistic achievements of others. The natural specimens, scientific equipment, archeological artifacts, religious relics, and pieces of art that were kept in Cabinets of Curiosity represented a wide variety of fields of study. These collections served as representations of the collector's wealth, wisdom, and power, as well as their intellectual aptitude and sense of wonder regarding the wider world.

Public Museums and the Organization of Scientific Knowledge During the Age of Enlightenment

One of the most significant turning points in the development of museums occurred in the 18th century during the Age of Enlightenment. It was around this time that the idea of granting the general public access to cultural and scientific collections started to gain traction. The Enlightenment was characterized by an emphasis on reason, knowledge, and education; one significant manifestation of this was the establishment of public museums. Carl Linnaeus, a Swedish botanist, was a significant individual who contributed significantly to the development of systematic classification systems. These systems laid the groundwork for the scientific organizing of museum collections. Both the British Museum in London, which was created in 1753, and the Louvre Museum in Paris, which was formed in 1793, are significant instances of public museums that originated during this century.

These museums are notable examples because they show the growing importance of making cultural and scientific items accessible to a wider public.

The Nineteenth Century: A Time of Discovery, Colonialism, and the Rise of Nationalism

The spirit of exploration, colonial expansion, and the formation of national identities all contributed to a boom in the founding of museums all over the world throughout the 19th century. This surge occurred during the century. As European powers expanded their reach to a variety of continents, explorers and anthropologists brought back a multitude of ethnographic and natural history collections, contributing to the diversity of museum holdings in the process. Museums became icons of colonial power and the acquisition of knowledge from far-off regions because they frequently displayed objects and specimens that were taken from territories that were under their control.

Simultaneously, the growth of nationalism inspired the establishment of museums that recognized and conserved the cultural heritage of individual nations. These museums were known as "heritage museums." The establishment of historical and art museums with the purpose of highlighting the accomplishments and history of a particular region or country was done with the intention of fostering a sense of pride and identification among the public. During this time period, there was a surge in popularity for the idea of museums acting as repositories of a nation's shared history and cultural identity.

This is the modern era, which is characterized by specialization, democratization, and digital transformation

Museums have undergone a remarkable process of democratization and diversity in the 20th and 21st centuries, with a rising emphasis placed on specialist collections, community participation, and technology innovation. More and more, museums are concentrating their collections and exhibitions on certain subjects. These topics might range anywhere from art and natural history to science, technology, and cultural heritage. For the purpose of catering to a wide variety of audiences and interests, specialized institutions such as scientific museums, children's museums, and memorial museums have come into existence.

In addition, the democratization of museums has resulted in an increased emphasis on accessibility and diversity in the museum-going experience. Museums have made it a priority to broaden their audience base by introducing educational programs, interactive exhibitions, and other forms of community service in an effort to make their collections and the knowledge contained within them more available to the general public. Efforts have been made to overcome barriers to access, such as the development of online collections, virtual tours, and other digital resources that enable audiences all over the world to engage with museum content via remote access.

The introduction of digital technology has resulted in a fundamental shift in the manner in which museums display and explain their collections. The visitor experience has been altered as a result of technological breakthroughs such as virtual reality, augmented reality, and interactive exhibitions. These advancements provide visitors chances to interact with museum content in ways that are immersive and engaging. Digital platforms have also helped to preserve and disseminate cultural heritage, making it possible for museums to communicate with audiences all over the world and breaking down geographical barriers in the process.

Trends and Obstacles Facing Our World Today

The history of museums and other cultural institutions has been affected in significant ways by a number of significant trends and problems that have emerged in the modern museum scene. The emphasis on community participation and co-curation, in which museums actively incorporate local communities in the process of generating exhibitions and programs, is one of the noteworthy developments that has been observed recently. This strategy encourages a feeling of ownership and inclusivity, so making it possible for a wide variety of voices and points of view to be expressed within museum settings.

In addition, there has been an increased emphasis placed on the ethical obligations of museums, specifically in relation to problems with the repatriation of cultural assets, restitution, and the decolonization of practices that are carried out in museums. A great number of institutions have begun conversations and partnerships with the communities from which their items originated in order to correct historical wrongs and guarantee the respectful management of cultural artifacts and human remains.

The issue of sustainability has also emerged as a key concern for museums, which has prompted campaigns to adopt techniques that are more environmentally friendly, lower carbon footprints, and increase environmental consciousness. Responsible exhibition practices, energy-efficient building designs, and the incorporation of environmental education into museum programming are some examples of the sustainable initiatives that museums are progressively adopting and implementing into their day-to-day operations.

In addition, in recent years there has been a growing awareness that museums play an important part in the promotion of social justice, diversity, and inclusivity. In recent years, a growing number of cultural institutions have embraced a more inclusive approach to narrative, making it a priority to include underrepresented voices and perspectives, disenfranchised populations, and various points of view in their exhibitions and collections. This commitment to social equity is evident in the development of exhibitions and activities that explore themes of race, gender, identity, and socioeconomic inequality. These topics are discussed in more detail below.

Museums continue to struggle with the difficulty of striking a balance between traditional preservation techniques and innovative approaches to public engagement in the face of increased globalization and improvements in technology. The transformation of museum experiences into digital ones has sparked conversations about the influence of technology on the genuine experience of visiting a museum and the place of real items in a world that is becoming more and more dominated by virtual reality. Museums are consistently working toward the goal of striking a balance between utilizing technological tools for the purposes of education and outreach and preserving the tactile and immersive aspects that give visitors a one-of-a-kind experience when they visit a museum.

The development of museums is illustrative of the ever-shifting dynamics of human civilization, cultural practices, and the body of human knowledge. From their humble beginnings as Cabinets of Curiosity to their current status as dynamic, accessible, and technologically savvy cultural institutions, museums have adapted to the varying demands and expectations of their audiences. This transformation occurred over the course of their history. As the 21st century progresses, museums are confronted with a whole new set of difficulties and opportunities, including the promotion of social justice and diversity, technologically driven innovation, ethical issues, and sustainable practices. The continuing appeal of museums as windows into history, art, and culture has not lessened over time, which bodes well for the dynamic continuation and development of these essential cultural institutions.

1.1 The origins of museums and galleries

Museums and galleries can be traced back to ancient civilizations, which placed a considerable emphasis on the protection of historical objects, religious relics, and historical records. These cultures were the forerunners of modern museums and galleries. The development of these institutions has been influenced in several ways, including by a wide variety of cultural practices and religious beliefs, as well as by a human tendency to preserve and exhibit artifacts that are historically, artistically, and scientifically significant. The human need to conserve, interpret, and pass down cultural heritage from one generation to the next can be better understood by gaining a better understanding of the early roots of museums and art galleries.

Origins & Collections from an Ancient Era

The ancient civilizations of Mesopotamia, Egypt, China, and the Indus Valley are where some of the earliest examples of cultural preservation can be discovered. It was in these ancient civilizations that rulers, religious leaders, and elites accumulated collections of rare objects, precious stones, and works of art. These early collections were used for a number of objectives, including the assertion of power and grandeur, religious worship, and royal patronage. Palaces, temples, and other colossal constructions were frequently used by these ancient cultures to showcase the riches and cultural achievements of their individual civilizations by displaying the goods that they had accumulated over the course of their history.

For example, in ancient Egypt, the practice of preserving funeral goods, mummies, and tomb paintings was closely tied to the belief in the afterlife as well as the necessity to provide a prosperous journey for the deceased in the world beyond. This was done in order to fulfill the requirement to ensure a prosperous voyage for the departed. The ornate tombs and burial chambers of pharaohs functioned as early repositories of cultural and historical artifacts. These tombs and chambers provided an insight into the creative and religious practices that were prevalent throughout that time period.

In a similar manner, the ancient Chinese emperors placed a strong emphasis on the preservation of cultural traditions and the pursuit of academic endeavors by amassing huge collections of artworks, calligraphy, and historical documents. These imperial collections not only served as a symbol of the ruler's authority, but they also helped to preserve Chinese art and culture and passed it down to subsequent generations.

Predecessors of the Renaissance and the Middle Ages

It was during the medieval and Renaissance centuries in Europe that the idea of collecting and presenting things of surprise and curiosity began to acquire importance; this is when the foundations of modern museums can be traced back to these time periods. The development of Cabinets of Curiosity, also known as Wunderkammer, signified a dramatic shift in the preservation and classification of natural specimens, scientific apparatus, and artistic marvels. Cabinets of Curiosity are also known by their German name, Wunderkammer. These private collections, which were frequently put together by wealthy academics, nobles, and naturalists, displayed an extensive variety of artifacts, some of which included unusual shells, minerals, taxidermy creatures, and ancient artifacts.

During the Renaissance, there was a resurgence of interest in classical education and an accompanying quest for knowledge. This interest led to the formation of private collections that attempted to replicate the intellectual activities of ancient intellectuals. The Medici family in Florence and the Habsburg family in Vienna both collected enormous art collections, which laid the framework for the formation of public museums in future centuries after their reigns. Not only did these collections honor the accomplishments of the past, but they also promoted a spirit of inquiry, investigation, and artistic creativity that would eventually change the cultural landscape of Europe. These collections can be found in countries all around Europe.

The Age of Enlightenment coincided with the beginning of the establishment of public museums

The 18th century was a pivotal era in the development of museums and galleries, since it saw the birth of public organizations that were committed to the conservation and presentation of cultural items.

This was a crucial turning point in the history of museums and galleries. The Enlightenment values of reason, information, and education were the driving forces behind the establishment of public museums. These museums' primary goals were to make art, historical artifacts, and scientific discoveries available to the general public. The British Museum was one of the earliest examples of a public organization that intended to house and present a vast array of cultural and historical items. It was established in London in 1753 and has been considered one of the world's preeminent museums ever since. Its holdings, which consisted of antiquities, specimens from natural history, and manuscripts, showed the increasing emphasis on the sharing of information and the promotion of public education.

The Louvre Museum in Paris, which opened in 1793 and played a major role in the democratization of art and culture by making the royal art collections available to the general people, was one of the first museums to be founded in the modern age. The transition of the Louvre from a royal palace to a public museum served as an illustrative example of the shift away from exclusive, private collections and toward inclusive, public institutions with the goal of fostering a sense of national identity and cultural pride.

Colonization Attempts and the Gathering of Ethnographic Materials

During the 19th and early 20th centuries, the expansion of colonial powers led to the acquisition of ethnographic collections from all over the world. The cultural items, indigenous artworks, and archaeological finds that came from Africa, Asia, the Americas, and the Pacific were amassed by European explorers, anthropologists, and colonial administrators. These artifacts, which were frequently obtained through imperial conquests and expeditions, were initially shown in ethnographic museums and colonial exhibitions, reflecting the Eurocentric viewpoint that was prevalent during that time period.

Although the early ethnographic collections were frequently selected through the lens of cultural imperialism and exoticism, they did help to preserve and chronicle native cultures and practices that could have otherwise been lost to history if they hadn't been collected. The ethical issues of presenting and interpreting these ethnographic collections are currently being faced by modern museums, which are working hard to convey a more inclusive and nuanced understanding of the myriad cultural identities and histories that exist in the world.

The Democratization of Culture and the Rise of Contemporary Museums

With the expansion of specialized institutions that are committed to art, history, science, technology, and cultural heritage, the 20th and 21st centuries have witnessed a democratization of museum culture. Museums have developed into dynamic, interactive environments that stress community engagement, educational outreach, and the promotion of diversity and inclusivity in their exhibits and programming.

They have embraced digital technology as well as new display tactics in order to produce experiences that are immersive as well as accessible for a variety of audiences.In addition, a reexamination of the origins and narratives of museum collections has been sparked as a result of the reevaluation of museum practices as well as the acknowledgment of the need for cultural restitution and decolonization. Numerous establishments are actively participating in discourse with the communities from which they obtained cultural objects, repatriating those items, and encouraging a more inclusive and fair depiction of cultural heritage within their exhibitions and other forms of programming.

1.2 Historical development and the changing purpose of museums

The historical growth of museums is a reflection of the shifting attitudes, values, and views that society has regarding the preservation of cultural heritage and information. Museums have undergone substantial alterations in their purpose and function throughout the course of their history. From their beginnings as private collections and Cabinets of Curiosities to their current roles as active educational institutions and cultural hubs, museums have come a long way. This in-depth investigation into the historical growth of museums will provide light on the developing societal attitudes that have affected the path that these cultural institutions have taken over the course of the ages.

The beginnings of everything, as well as the curio cabinet

Cabinets of Curiosity, often referred to as Wunderkammer, were created during the Renaissance period in Europe to display a wide variety of natural specimens, rare objects, and artistic marvels. These early museums may be dated back to the Renaissance period in Europe. These private collections functioned as stores of wonder and knowledge, expressing the intellectual curiosity and the desire to organize and understand the natural world around them. The Cabinets of Curiosity were frequently used as symbols of riches, social prestige, and the quest of knowledge. They demonstrated the collector's diverse interests and intellectual prowess through the display of various artifacts.

The Age of Enlightenment coincided with the development of public museums

The Age of Enlightenment in the 18th century represented a fundamental shift in the aim and function of museums, with the establishment of public institutions committed to the dissemination of information and the advancement of public education. This transformation occurred concurrently with the beginning of the modern museum movement. Denis Diderot and Jean le Rond d'Alembert were two influential people who championed the values of reason, critical inquiry, and intellectual enlightenment. As a result of their efforts, the framework was laid for the formation of public museums as accessible sites for learning and cultural enrichment.

MUSEUMS AND GALLERIES

Both the British Museum in London, which was created in 1753, and the Louvre Museum in Paris, which was formed in 1793, typified the Enlightenment's emphasis on the democratization of cultural heritage and the accessibility of art and historical items to the general people. The British Museum was established in 1753, while the Louvre Museum was established in 1793. These public museums acted as stores of cultural memory, so contributing to the development of a sense of national identity and cultural pride while simultaneously nurturing the values of knowledge diffusion and intellectual inquiry.

The role that nationalism and colonialism played in the formation of cultural identities

In the 19th century, when nations tried to show their cultural identity and supremacy through the preservation and display of historical objects, museums became intertwined with the forces of nationalism and colonialism. This is because museums preserve and display historical items. The establishment of museums came to play an important role in the formation of national narratives and the promotion of a sense of collective memory and shared heritage among the general population. The establishment of history museums and national galleries served the purpose of honoring the accomplishments and historical legacies of particular areas or countries, so bolstering the concept of a unified national identity that was founded on the nation's collective history.

Concurrently, the development of European colonial powers resulted in the acquisition of ethnographic collections from all over the world. These collections contributed to the diversification of museum holdings and the representation of a wide range of cultural traditions from across the world. However, these early ethnographic collections were frequently selected through the prism of cultural imperialism and exoticism. This reflects the Eurocentric viewpoints that were dominant during the time period of colonial exploration and conquest.

The Turning Point Towards Education and Involvement in the Community in the 20th Century

The 20th century was characterized by a substantial shift in the aim of museums, with an increased emphasis placed on educational outreach, community participation, and the democratization of cultural experiences. Museums started placing a greater emphasis on public programming, interactive displays, and educational projects with the goal of promoting a more in-depth comprehension of art, history, and science among a wider variety of audience types. The significance of unstructured education and participatory activities in museum settings is becoming increasingly acknowledged, as seen by the proliferation of museums devoted specifically to the fields of science and technology as well as the education of young people.

Additionally, the second half of the 20th century witnessed a reevaluation of museum practices, with a greater emphasis on inclusivity, diversity, and the representation of underrepresented voices within museum narratives. This was a significant shift from the practices of the earlier part of the century. The necessity for cultural restitution, decolonization, and the respectful representation of multiple cultural identities within their collections and exhibitions was recognized by museums, and these institutions started engaging in discourse with the communities from whom their artifacts originated.

Technologies, inclusiveness, and social responsibility are examples of contemporary trends

In the 21st century, museums are continuously adapting in order to meet the difficulties and opportunities posed by globalization, digital innovation, and the requirement for a higher level of social responsibility. The use of technology such as virtual reality, augmented reality, and interactive displays has altered the experience that museum visitors have while visiting the institution. These technologies enable options for involvement with the museum's content that are both immersive and accessible. The proliferation of digital platforms has made it possible for museums to attract visitors from all over the world, to transcend geographic borders, and to stimulate cultural debate and exchange on a global scale.

In addition, modern museums have placed a significant emphasis on inclusiveness, diversity, and social justice in their efforts to portray a more comprehensive and equitable narrative of cultural heritage that incorporates a variety of viewpoints and experiences. These museums are attempting to represent a more complete and equitable account of cultural heritage. Numerous establishments are actively participating in community-based projects, collaborative exhibitions, and outreach activities, all of which have the goal of fostering discussion, understanding, and empathy among various communities.

In addition, the 21st century has witnessed a greater emphasis placed on the social and environmental responsibilities of museums, with many establishments embracing environmentally sustainable methods, promoting environmental awareness, and pushing for social justice and equity. Museums have evolved into forums for discussing topical topics such as climate change, human rights, and cultural diversity. In doing so, they are helping to cultivate a feeling of global citizenship and social responsibility in the individuals who visit them.

The historical development of museums is a reflection of the changing views of society toward cultural heritage, the diffusion of knowledge, and community engagement. From their humble beginnings as cabinets of curiosities and private collections to their present-day roles as active educational institutions and centers of cultural activity, museums have evolved to meet the shifting requirements and goals of a wide variety of audiences. Highlighting the transformational power of museums as forums for education, discourse, and the celebration of cultural variety, the present trends in museum practices indicate an increasing emphasis on technology-driven innovation, inclusivity, and social responsibility.

1.3 Key figures and milestones in the history of museums

MUSEUMS AND GALLERIES

The history of museums is filled with significant personalities and landmarks that have played a key role in the growth and development of museums as cultural institutions throughout the course of many decades, centuries, and millennia. This investigation will look into the essential personalities and significant events that have made an indelible imprint on the history of museums. These persons and events range from pioneering collectors and curators to visionary founders and revolutionary moments.

Figures of Critical Importance to the Development of Museums

Sir Hans Sloane, who lived from 1660 until 1753: Sloane, a British physician and naturalist, is credited with laying the groundwork for the British Museum with his extensive collection of natural history specimens, antiquities, and books. His legacy of more than 71,000 items to the country formed the foundation for what is now one of the most well-known public museums in the whole wide world.

Denis Diderot (1713-1784) wrote the following: Diderot was a notable Enlightenment philosopher and writer. He was also a co-editor of the enormous book known as the "Encyclopédie," which exemplified the ethos of the Enlightenment and helped to the spread of knowledge and ideas. His efforts to ensure that the general people have access to information were critical to the establishment of public museums.

Charles Willson Peale was born in 1741 and died in 1827. Peale was an American artist and naturalist who is recognized for founding Peale's Museum, which is considered to be one of the first public museums in the United States. His idea of teaching the public through a diverse selection of exhibitions and educational programs provided the groundwork for the long-standing legacy of museums in the United States.

Sir Richard Owen, who lived from 1804 till 1892: Owen, a British paleontologist and anatomist, was instrumental in the formation of the Natural History Museum in London. Owen was also a pioneer in the field of anatomy. The direction that natural history museums have taken as a result of his contributions to the study of extinct species and the taxonomy of animals has been substantially influenced.

Henrietta Johnston (1674–1729) is acknowledged for her role in preserving the cultural legacy of colonial America through her work as an early American portrait artist. Johnston lived from 1674 until 1729. Her portraits add to the historical story of early American painting while also providing interesting insights into the social and cultural climate of the time period in which she lived.

Significant Events in the Development of Museums

The Capitoline Museums were established in 1471 by Pope Sixtus IV and are regarded as the world's oldest public museums. They are located in Rome. They display the concept of a repository of cultural heritage that is open to the public by housing a remarkable collection of ancient art and artifacts and making them available to the public.

The Ashmolean Museum (1683): The Ashmolean Museum in Oxford, which was founded by Elias Ashmole, is frequently recognized as the world's first university museum. The museum was established in 1683. It heralded a dramatic shift in the purpose of museums, which shifted from being private collections to becoming organizations dedicated to education and the promotion of knowledge.

The Louvre in Paris, which was formerly used as a royal palace, was converted into a public museum during the French Revolution in the year 1793. It was a defining milestone in the movement toward the democratization of art and the founding of public museums as places of cultural enrichment that were open to the general public.

The Bequest of Sir Hans Sloane to the Nation and the Subsequent founding of the British Museum (1753): The bequest that Sir Hans Sloane made to the nation and the subsequent founding of the British Museum constituted an important milestone in the history of public museums. It established a standard for the public's access to collections of cultural artifacts and natural history specimens.

The Museum of Modern Art (often known as MoMA) was established in 1929: The Museum of Modern Art in New York City, which was co-founded by Abby Aldrich Rockefeller and two other women, was a driving force behind the widespread acceptance of modern and contemporary art. Its unconventional approach to showcasing artwork and teaching the general audience established brand-new benchmarks for art museums all around the world.

The First Meeting of the International Council of Museums (ICOM) Was Held in 1946: ICOM is an international organization that was established in the aftermath of World War II with the purpose of fostering collaboration and maintaining professional standards among museums all over the world. It has been a significant contributor to the establishment of ethical standards for museum practices and the promotion of international cooperation.

The emergence of Virtual Museums in the Late 20th Century Due to the proliferation of digital technology, the late 20th century saw the creation of virtual museums, which allow users from all over the world to access and investigate museum collections online.

With the passing of this significant milestone, museums have become more accessible to audiences all across the world.

The Saga of the Elgin Marbles, which spanned the 19th and 20th centuries: The Elgin Marbles are ancient Greek sculptures that were removed from the Parthenon and are currently housed at the British Museum. The dispute over the ownership and repatriation of the Elgin Marbles has brought to light the ethical concerns that are associated with the purchase and display of cultural items. This debate has added fuel to the fire of the current conversation concerning the repatriation of cultural heritage.

Transformational Moments in Museum History: Milestones

The Enlightenment Era Laid the Groundwork for the Development of Public Museums The Enlightenment Era, which was distinguished by the pursuit of reason, knowledge, and intellectual inquiry, was essential in laying the groundwork for the development of public museums. It was a watershed moment in the evolution of the cultural landscape, marking the transition from private collections to cultural institutions open to the public.

Colonial Expansion and the Beginning of Ethnographic Collections During the 19th century, European powers engaged in colonial expansion, which resulted in the acquisition of ethnographic collections from all over the world. These collections not only contributed to the rich diversity of the museum's holdings, but they also sparked ethical debates regarding cultural imperialism and the appropriateness of museum displays.

The Turn Towards Education and Inclusivity That Happened in the 20th Century: Education, participation in the local community, and the advancement of inclusiveness all had a significant role in the transformation that took place in the mission of museums during the 20th century. Museums started placing a greater emphasis on public programming and interactive exhibitions, which helped audiences from a variety of backgrounds get a deeper understanding of art, history, and science.

Technology and the Digital Transformation of Museums The incorporation of technology into museums, in particular in the form of virtual exhibits and interactive displays, has completely transformed the experience that museum visitors have while also increasing the availability of museum collections. It marks a watershed point in the way that technology may be used to revolutionize the ways in which learning and engagement are fostered.

The Continuous Conversation Regarding Cultural Repatriation and Decolonization: The 21st century has witnessed a growing awareness of the necessity for cultural restitution and the decolonization of museum practices. This has been one of the most significant developments in the field. The continuous conversation on topics such as repatriation, restitution, and the fair depiction of multiple cultural identities represents a watershed moment in the ethical obligations of museums.

The evolution of museums, as well as the reasons for their existence, have been profoundly influenced by a number of pivotal people and watershed moments that are interspersed throughout their histories. These individuals and events have contributed to the development of museums as platforms for education, cultural enrichment, and the preservation of cultural heritage. From the early collectors and researchers who accumulated Cabinets of Curiosity to the founders of public museums, these individuals and events have played a role in the growth of museums. The ongoing significance of museums in generating cultural narratives and developing a deeper awareness of the world in which we live is reflected in the ways in which these institutions are adapting their functions and giving greater attention to ethical concerns in the 21st century.

1.4 The impact of technology on modern museums

In this day and age of digital advancement, technology has emerged as an indispensable and game-changing factor in the world of contemporary museums. The power of technology has been used by museums in order to increase visitor engagement, improve educational opportunities, and broaden access to cultural artifacts. This investigation will look into the varied impact that technology has had on contemporary museums. It will shed light on how digital innovation has transformed the experience of museum visitors, as well as curatorial practices and the preservation and dissemination of cultural items.

The Impact of Digital Innovation on the Experience of Visitors

Virtual Reality (VR) and Augmented Reality (AR): The technology behind virtual reality and augmented reality have transformed the method in which visitors engage with museum collections. Virtual reality (VR) provides users with an experience that is multisensory and interactive. Users are able to immerse themselves in historical and artistic settings. AR superimposes digital information on the real environment, giving viewers access to supplementary information, 3D reconstructions, and multimedia content connected to the exhibits they are viewing. Virtual reality (VR) and augmented reality (AR) have been blended into exhibitions at museums in order to create immersive narrative experiences. These experiences allow visitors to go into the past, investigate historical civilizations, and interact with virtual artifacts.

The interactive displays, touchscreens, and hands-on exhibits that have become standard fare in contemporary museums are known together as "interactive exhibits." It doesn't matter whether it's a scientific experiment, an artistic production, or a historical simulation; these exhibits inspire viewers to actively engage with the information in some way. The use of interactive components makes education more engaging and approachable for students of varying ages and learning preferences. They provide an active, interactive experience that encourages participation and goes beyond the conventional passive observation.

Apps for mobile devices have advanced to the point that they can now provide in-depth information, audio commentary, and multimedia content to go along with exhibitions. This is a significant development from the traditional audio guides that were used in the past. Visitors can explore the exhibits at their own leisure using their own cellphones or gadgets provided by the museum. This allows them to obtain deeper insights into the art, history, or science that is being displayed. The users of these apps also have the ability to personalize their experience by selecting from a variety of languages and gaining access to a wide variety of accessibility features.

The concept of gamification has been adopted by museums, and many have begun incorporating parts of games into their displays as well as their programming. Educational games have also gained popularity. Educational games present visitors with challenges that require them to solve puzzles, provide answers to questions, and investigate topical topics. Learning is made more exciting and engaging through gamified experiences, which also encourage a spirit of healthy competition and open-ended exploration among attendees.

The usage of social media platforms has enabled museums to connect with audiences all around the world. Digital sharing has also become increasingly popular. On social media sites such as Instagram, Twitter, and Facebook, visitors are prompted to talk about their travels and post images along with their reflections. The use of digital word-of-mouth marketing helps museums reach a wider audience and gives visitors a stronger sense of belonging to a community. The use of hashtags and content generated by visitors is becoming an essential component of museum promotion and interaction.

Virtual Tours and Online Collections: Many museums now provide virtual tours and online collections, which allow visitors to view their objects and exhibitions from a distance. Users are able to examine museum exhibits and artifacts without leaving the comfort of their own homes thanks to virtual tours, which frequently include photographs captured in 360 degrees and in-depth descriptions. Because of advancements in technology, people who do not live near museums or do not have the time to travel there now have easier access to the world's cultural treasures.

Curation and preservation of digital content

The usage of paper cataloging systems has given way to digital databases at museums, which have allowed for the institution's transition away from those methods. The maintaining of records, the preservation of information, and the retrieval of information about objects can all be made more efficient through the use of digital cataloging. Additionally, it makes it possible for museums to make their holdings accessible to a larger audience through the use of online catalogs.

The area of conservation and restoration has been completely shaken up by the introduction of digital technologies in recent years. Conservators are able to examine and repair artworks with a higher level of precision because to the implementation of advanced imaging techniques such as 3D scanning, multispectral imaging, and digital mapping. These technologies also help in the discovery of hidden details, which can shed light on previously unknown information regarding the creative process as well as the background of the artwork.

Preventative conservation involves the use of environmental monitoring systems at museums, which are often comprised of sensors and digital controls. These systems assist museums in maintaining stable conditions for their collections. These systems control the environment in terms of temperature, humidity, and lighting in order to protect artifacts from being damaged or deteriorating. The use of digital monitoring allows for modifications to be made in real time, which both protects the environment and lowers the danger of damage.

The use of digital platforms by curators to convey engaging stories about the items in their collections is referred to as "digital storytelling." Museums now have the ability to interact with a larger audience and tell the stories that are behind the objects through the use of virtual exhibitions, documentaries, and online galleries. The use of this digital storytelling approach brings the objects to life in new ways and improves the overall experience for the visitors.

Reach Across the Globe and Attempts at Cultural Negotiation

worldwide Cooperation As a result of technological advancements, museums are now able to participate in worldwide cooperation and cultural exchange. It is possible for museums to lend other institutions from all around the world their collections, expertise, and exhibitions. This collaboration encourages the sharing of knowledge and ideas on a worldwide scale, as well as a greater understanding between different cultures.

Digital Repatriation and the Preservation of Cultural Heritage: Museums are becoming increasingly involved in digital repatriation programs, in which they share digital records and reproductions of artifacts with the communities from whom they originated.

Concerns regarding the repatriation of cultural assets and the preservation of indigenous knowledge can be addressed more effectively with the assistance of this collaborative approach.

Concerns and Things to Take Into Account

Inequality in the Digital Age: The fact that not all guests have the same level of access to technology or the internet can lead to differences in their experiences in museums. To ensure that everyone can enjoy their experience, museums need to address the digital divide.

Museums are required to handle the data they collect from visitors in a responsible manner and safeguard it from any potential cyber dangers. Strong data security measures are required because of the collecting of personally identifiable information through the use of applications and interactive exhibits.

The application of digital technology, such as touchscreen screens, may have certain effects on the surrounding environment. The benefits of technology must be balanced with the museum's commitment to environmentally responsible operations.

Authenticity and reproductions: The usage of digital reproductions and augmented reality can potentially cause visitors to wonder whether or not they are participating in an authentic museum experience. It is a difficult issue to find a happy medium between the use of technology and the protection of the tangible, authentic, and original qualities of artifacts.

Ethical Considerations Regarding Technology Museums are obligated to give serious thought to the ethical ramifications of incorporating technology into their displays. There is the potential for bias in digital storytelling, which can give rise to ethical dilemmas about issues such as cultural appropriation, the representation of sensitive topics, and the possibility of bias.

The Prospects for the Future of Museums in the Age of Technology

Artificial Intelligence (AI): AI has the potential to improve the overall experience for visitors by providing personalized suggestions, chatbots that can answer inquiries, and even the generation of AI-generated artwork. Automating particular museum tasks like visitor statistics and artifact cataloging might also be possible with the help of artificial intelligence.

Big Data and Analytics: Big data and analytics provide museums with the opportunity to gather insights into the behavior and preferences of museum visitors. This information can be used to inform the design of the display, the creation of content, and marketing initiatives.

Extended Reality (XR) refers to the combination of virtual reality (VR), augmented reality (AR), and mixed reality (MR) in order to give visitors with experiences that are even more engaging and immersive. It is possible that XR technologies may become easier to use and more extensively implemented in museums.

The use of blockchain technology allows for the protection of artworks and artifacts while also allowing their provenance to be independently validated. This technology has the potential to raise the level of confidence and transparency in the art market and the process of acquiring cultural treasures.

Education through Digital Means It is anticipated that educational programs will increasingly make use of digital technologies in the coming years. It is possible for museums to provide students of all ages with virtual classrooms, online courses, and other types of interactive learning experiences.

Technology will play a major role in enhancing the global connectivity of museums, which is important for both the practice of cultural diplomacy and for globalization more generally. The exchange of collections and information between institutions all over the world will enhance the cause of cultural diplomacy and understanding between people of different backgrounds.

Chapter 2

Types of Museums and Galleries

Museums and art galleries play an important role in maintaining and presenting a wide variety of cultural, historical, and artistic artifacts. In this way, they act as stewards of our shared human history. The contributions that these institutions provide to the preservation of tangible and intangible legacy, the promotion of cultural understanding, and the delivery of educational opportunities to people of varying ages and walks of life are indispensable. There is a wide variety of museum and gallery formats to be found all over the world; each format serves a particular function and caters to a specific set of interests and fields of study. This in-depth study will investigate the various kinds of museums and galleries, illuminating the distinctive characteristics, purposes, and contributions that each type of institution makes to society.

1. Galleries and Museums of Visual Arts
   Museums and galleries dedicated to showcasing works of art are likely the most well-known and well recognized kind of cultural institution. They are experts in the collecting, preserving, and exhibiting of many different types of visual art, including paintings, sculptures, photography, and other types of visual art forms. In many cases, these establishments are home to vast art collections spanning a wide variety of eras and genres, including anything from ancient and Renaissance art to current and contemporary pieces. Not only do museums and galleries illustrate the aesthetic development of human creativity, but they also provide a platform for artists to present their work and contribute to the larger discourse on the relevance of art in society. This is one of the many reasons why art museums and galleries are so important.
2. Museums Dedicated to the Past
   Museums of history are institutions that are committed to preserving and presenting the historical narrative of various communities, societies, and civilizations. They display a wide variety of artifacts, records, and interactive exhibits

that provide insights into the social, political, economic, and cultural elements of particular eras and locations throughout history. These museums provide a broad overview of the past, ranging from ancient civilizations and medieval ages to the industrial revolution and modern history. This enables visitors to connect with their roots and comprehend the advancement of human communities over time.

3. Museums Dedicated to Natural History

   The study and presentation of the natural world is the primary focus of natural history museums. This includes the fields of geology, paleontology, zoology, botany, and ecology, among others. They are home to enormous collections of specimens, fossils, and displays that highlight the development of life on Earth, the diversity of varied ecosystems, and the relationships between various species and the settings in which they live. The goal of educational programs and interactive exhibits at natural history museums is to raise awareness about the environment and encourage people to participate in conservation efforts. These museums also attempt to bring attention to the significance of preserving biodiversity and natural resources.

4. Science Centers and Museums

   Science museums are institutions that are committed to advancing scientific literacy and comprehension by means of hands-on displays, live demonstrations, and structured educational programming. They encompass a broad spectrum of scientific fields, such as physics, chemistry, biology, astronomy, and technology. In science museums, visitors are generally encouraged to participate in the process of discovery via the use of hands-on activities and experiments. These activities and experiments encourage visitors to investigate scientific concepts and phenomena in an atmosphere that is both exciting and interesting. These establishments play a significant part in igniting a love of science in individuals of all ages and paving the way for the next generation of scientists and innovators to come into the world.

5. Museums Catering to Children

   The educational and recreational requirements of children are carefully considered during the planning stages of a children's museum's construction. These museums have hands-on exhibits, designated play areas, and educational programs that foster an atmosphere conducive to learning through exploration and play. Children's museums strive to create a lifetime appreciation for learning and cultural enrichment in children by introducing them to a variety of hands-on experiences and activities that are geared toward their age group. This encourages children to be inquisitive, creative, and analytical thinkers.

6. Museums Specializing in Archaeology

   Archaeological museums are establishments that are dedicated to the conservation and exhibition of archaeological objects and discoveries. These museums provide insights into the society, cultures, and civilizations that existed in the past. In most cases, these establishments are in possession of a wide variety of excavated objects, like as pottery, tools, artwork, and architectural relics. These artifacts offer significant insight into the ways of life, practices, and accomplishments of bygone civilizations. The interpretation of historical narratives and the promotion of archaeological research are two of the most important roles that archaeological museums perform, and both of these roles contribute to our understanding of human history and the development of cultural traditions.

7. Museums With a Particular Focus

   Specialized museums concentrate their attention on certain ideas, topics, or fields of study; they serve specific audiences with collections and exhibitions that are tailored to their particular interests. It's possible that these museums will focus on certain subjects, such as technology, aviation, maritime history, textiles, or unique cultural practices. These museums give in-depth insights and extensive perspectives on specific themes by concentrating on specialized areas of study or interest. They cater to enthusiasts, researchers, and scholars who have a deep interest in particular fields of study or cultural traditions.

8. Online Museums and Galleries

Virtual museums have evolved as an innovative technique to preserving and showcasing cultural history as well as artistic accomplishments as digital technology has advanced. By utilizing online galleries, interactive multimedia content, and virtual tours, visitors of these digital platforms are given the opportunity to investigate museum collections, exhibits, and artifacts. Individuals from all parts of the world are now able to interact with artistic expressions and cultural heritage because to the accessibility provided by virtual museums, which make cultural resources and educational materials available to everyone. This is possible because virtual museums are not limited by physical space or geographical location.

Museums and art galleries play an essential role in cultural preservation, education, and enrichment, and they provide important contributions to our overall understanding of human history, the arts, and the sciences. Each sort of museum, from art museums and history museums to natural history museums and specialized institutions, plays a distinct part in the process of conserving and presenting a variety of dimensions of human culture and knowledge. This includes museums of history, art, and natural history. These institutions continue to excite and educate audiences by encouraging appreciation, curiosity, and comprehension. This helps to ensure that the rich tapestry of human legacy will continue to be accessible and relevant for centuries to come.

2.1 Art museums and galleries

A Feast for the Eyes: How Art Galleries and Museums Celebrate the Creativity and Expression of Humans

Art museums and galleries serve as guiding lights for artistic appreciation, cultural enrichment, and historical preservation. They capture the essence of human ingenuity and expression across the years in a way that is both timeless and timeless. These establishments act as registries of artistic accomplishments; they store a wide variety of paintings, sculptures, photographs, and other forms of visual art that exemplify the vibrant tapestry of human imagination and invention. These organizations serve as repositories of artistic achievements. Art museums and art galleries give a platform for artists to express their creativity and contribute to a wider conversation on the relevance of art in society. This platform can range from classical masterpieces to modern works of art and includes everything in between.

The Development of Art Galleries and Museums Throughout History

The notion of art museums may be traced back to ancient civilizations, where royal collections and private galleries acted as repositories of creative and cultural treasures. These early civilizations laid the groundwork for the modern concept of art museums. However, the modern concept of public art museums did not come into existence until the Enlightenment period in Europe. This was a result of a growing interest in preserving and presenting cultural items for the instruction and entertainment of the general public. The founding of the Louvre Museum in Paris in the latter half of the 18th century was a crucial turning point in the evolution of public art institutions. It also served as a model for the later proliferation of art museums and galleries all over the world.

The Practices of Curators and the Caretaking of Collections

There are specialists known as curators and art historians who are employed by art museums and galleries. These individuals are in charge of the organization, preservation, and interpretation of art collections. The research, documentation, and conservation work that goes into curatorial techniques have to be extremely thorough since the integrity of the artwork and its historical context must be preserved at all costs. In order to purchase, present, and interpret works of art, curators frequently engage in collaboration with researchers, artists, and collectors. This helps to contribute to a thorough understanding of art movements, styles, and cultural influences.

The process of collection curation involves the employment of strategic acquisition tactics. These involve the careful selection of artworks by museum curators that are in line with the institution's goal and the focus of its thematic research. This method takes into account aspects like as the work's historical significance, artistic excellence, and cultural significance. As a result, the museum's collection is guaranteed to have a wide-ranging and thorough representation of artistic expressions originating from a variety of time periods and civilizations.

Exhibition Areas and Associated Interpretive Procedures

Art galleries and museums typically provide dynamic exhibition spaces that have been thoughtfully planned to improve the degree to which visitors engage with the artworks that are on view. These places have been carefully selected to present visitors with an experience that is both transforming and immersive. Examples of these spaces include expansive galleries with natural lighting and small rooms that provide an atmosphere conducive to contemplation. The curators of an exhibition use a variety of interpretative practices, such as informative plaques, audio guides, and interactive displays, to provide insights into the historical context, artistic techniques, and thematic interpretations of the artworks. This helps to foster a deeper appreciation and understanding of the artistic process as well as the cultural significance of the exhibition.

Programs for Education, as well as Involvement in the Community

Art museums and galleries play an active role in the community by, in addition to hosting exhibitions, providing educational programs and community engagement projects with the goals of fostering an appreciation for the arts, increased cultural awareness, and more creative expression. These programs offer a variety of activities, such as guided tours, workshops, lectures, and outreach events, aimed at appealing to a wide range of audiences, including students, families, and art enthusiasts. Art museums and galleries attempt to establish an inclusive and accessible atmosphere that stimulates dialogue, critical thinking, and creative discovery in order to foster a stronger connection between the general public and the world of art. They do this by cultivating a culture of learning and engagement, which encourages visitors to engage with the institution's exhibitions and programs.

Fostering Intercultural Communication and Discussion Across the World

Museums and galleries of art act as catalysts for cultural exchange and worldwide dialogue. They make it easier for people to talk about their artistic experiences with one another and create a deeper knowledge of a variety of cultural points of view. These institutions encourage cross-cultural appreciation and collaboration by participating in international partnerships, traveling exhibitions, and cultural exchange programs. By doing so, they are able to transcend geographical barriers while simultaneously developing mutual respect and understanding across many cultures and societies. Art museums and galleries contribute to the enrichment of global cultural heritage and the promotion of cultural diplomacy by showcasing artworks from a variety of cultures and regions. This places an emphasis on the universal language of art as a means of transcending cultural differences and fostering connections among people from a variety of backgrounds.

Keeping the Artistic Legacy Alive and Serving as an Inspiration to Future Generations

The safeguarding of artistic heritage for succeeding generations is one of the most important roles that art museums and galleries play in their communities. These organizations preserve the lifespan and integrity of art collections by engaging in careful conservation techniques and initiating archival efforts. This protects the art collections from the deterioration caused by environmental factors as well as the passage of time. Art museums and galleries inspire future generations to embrace creativity, innovation, and artistic expression by preserving the artistic heritage of past and contemporary artists. This nurtures a legacy of cultural enrichment and artistic excellence that transcends temporal boundaries and continues to shape the artistic landscape for years to come. Art museums and galleries are a vital part of the artistic landscape.

Art museums and galleries play an important role as stewards of cultural history. They encourage a profound appreciation for the arts and make significant contributions to the expansion of human civilization.

These organizations serve a key role in maintaining artistic heritage, stimulating cultural debate, and inspiring creative expression across a wide variety of cultures and generations through their curatorial practices, educational initiatives, and cultural exchange programs. Art museums and galleries, as foundations of artistic appreciation and cultural enlightenment, continue to define the story of human creativity and serve as enduring testaments to the transformative power of art in society. Art museums and galleries have been around for a long time.

2.2 Natural history museums

Discovering the Extraordinary Web of Life on Earth Is What Natural History Museums Do Best

The tale of life on our world over the past can be found preserved in natural history museums, which serve as treasuries for the astounding variety of life on our planet. These institutions act as bridges between human understanding and the natural world, providing a unique opportunity to investigate and enjoy the wondrous aspects of the natural world. An astonishing variety of artifacts that give information on Earth's evolutionary history, biodiversity, and ecological interconnections can be found in the collections of natural history museums. These artifacts range from ancient fossils to intricately preserved specimens.

The Development of Natural History Museums Throughout History

The Age of Enlightenment was a time period that was characterized by intellectual curiosity as well as the desire to carefully classify and understand the natural world. This goal led to the development of natural history museums during this time period. Scholars and naturalists have created specimen collections, including things like minerals, fossils, and plant specimens, in order to make the study of the flora and fauna of Earth more accessible. These collections, which were amassed over the course of time, eventually gave rise to the establishment of museums that were committed to the conservation and exhibition of artifacts relating to the natural world.

The 19th century saw a surge in the establishment of natural history museums, which developed in tandem with the expansion of scientific fields such as geology, paleontology, botany, and zoology. These museums played an essential part in cultivating a deep appreciation for the variety of life on Earth and stimulating the interchange of knowledge as scientific understanding and exploration progressed over time.

The Practices of Curators and the Caretaking of Collections

The organization, upkeep, and interpretation of a museum's collection are the purview of its curators and scientists, who are employed by the museum to carry out these duties. A comprehensive knowledge of the specimens and the historical setting in which they were collected is required for the curation procedure. The lifetime of specimens and the preservation of their scientific value are dependent on the study, documenting, and conservation activities that are carried out by curators.

The curation of a collection is a painstaking process that involves careful planning for both the purchase and storage of items. The museum's curators are responsible for selecting specimens that fit in with the institution's mission, its goals for scientific research, and its educational goals. This method ensures that the collection at the museum is representative of a wide variety of species and ecosystems, which helps to create an in-depth understanding of the biodiversity and evolution of the Earth.

Exhibition Areas and Associated Interpretive Procedures

The compelling exhibition rooms that natural history museums provide let visitors feel as though they have been transported into the natural world. These areas have been meticulously planned to provide visitors with an immersive experience. This can be accomplished through the use of dioramas that show various ecosystems, interactive exhibits, or multimedia presentations. Visitors are able to deepen their understanding of the ecological interconnections, evolutionary processes, and scientific discoveries that have contributed to our current perspective of the natural world through the use of interpretative activities.

Contextual information and scientific explanations are offered through the use of informational signage, labeling, audio tours, and interactive exhibits, which together provide a thorough comprehension of the exhibits. The introduction of cutting-edge technology and immersive experiences, such as virtual reality or augmented reality, can boost the engagement of visitors and the educational value of these museums, allowing visitors to explore ecosystems and animals in a way that has never been possible before.

Programs for Education, as well as Involvement in the Community

The advancement of scientific literacy, increased environmental consciousness, and a more in-depth comprehension of the natural world are the goals that natural history museums strive to achieve. Educational activities and initiatives that promote community engagement are extremely important to the success of this undertaking. These programs frequently consist of guided tours, talks, seminars, and other types of outreach activities that are geared for a wide variety of participants, including students, families, nature enthusiasts, and researchers. These museums cultivate a connection between the general people and the natural world by promoting a culture of learning and participation in their own communities.

In addition, many museums of natural history provide educational resources for use in classrooms and other educational settings. These resources contribute to the spread of scientific information and the incorporation of natural history ideas into educational programs. They contribute to the overarching goal of inspiring a new generation of naturalists and environmental stewards by acting in this manner, which is a significant contribution.

Increasing Environmental Consciousness While Working to Preserve It

Natural history museums play an important part in raising people's awareness of environmental issues and supporting efforts to conserve them. They address critical environmental concerns like climate change, the loss of habitat, and species conservation through educational programs and displays. These organizations encourage tourists to become champions for environmental protection and responsible stewardship of the Earth's resources by displaying the beauty and fragility of the natural world.

In addition, natural history museums frequently participate in research and frequently work in conjunction with conservation organizations and scientists in order to contribute to ongoing efforts to preserve biodiversity and protect endangered species. These institutions develop a deeper awareness of the vital role that humans play in the preservation of the planet's ecosystems by providing support for scientific study and communicating the findings of that research.

Protecting the Rich Biological Heritage of Our Planet

Museums of natural history play a vital role as key repositories of the biological heritage of the Earth. They protect the specimens from the deterioration caused by the environment and the passage of time by adhering to stringent conservation standards and participating in archival activities. These collections are extremely helpful to scientists that study evolution, ecology, and biodiversity since they serve as a reference for subsequent research and as a foundation for studies of taxonomy.

There are instances in which natural history museums hold collections that contain specimens that are either extinct, extremely uncommon, or of vital relevance to scientific research. These specimens are an essential resource for gaining a knowledge of how the ecosystems of the Earth are adapting to their changing conditions because they provide invaluable insights into the past, present, and future of our planet's biodiversity.

The incredible web of life on Earth can be better understood through visits to natural history museums, which serve as portals to the wondrous aspects of our home planet. These institutions play a crucial role in creating environmental consciousness, scientific understanding, and a profound respect for the diversity and interconnectivity of the natural world through their curatorial practices, educational programs, and conservation activities. This is accomplished through the various ways in which they engage in conservation efforts. Natural history museums, in their role as custodians of the Earth's biological legacy, continue to pique visitors' interests and motivate them to be good stewards of the environment. This helps to ensure that the splendor and importance of the natural world will continue to be appreciated by both the current generation and the generations to come.

2.3 Science and technology museums

Museums of science and technology serve as immersive gateways to the ever-expanding fields of scientific research and technological advancement. These institutions serve as a link between the complex world of science and the general public by providing enthralling exhibitions and engaging displays that shed light on the mysteries of the cosmos, the wonders of technological advancements, and the significant role they play in shaping our day-to-day lives. Science and technology museums serve as a stimulus for scientific curiosity, creativity, and a greater understanding of the ever-evolving world of science and technology. Exhibits at science and technology museums can range from state-of-the-art displays on space exploration to historical artifacts of early industrial revolutions.

Museums Documenting the Development of Science and Technology Throughout History

The development of science and technology museums can be traced back to the latter half of the 19th century and the early part of the 20th century. This was a time period that was characterized by rapid industrialization, the expansion of technology, and an increasing interest with the promise of science and technology. Early exhibits frequently concentrated on lauding the accomplishments brought about by the Industrial Revolution and the advancement of technology. These early displays highlighted the machines, inventions, and breakthroughs that had significantly impacted the fields of transportation, communication, and manufacturing.

The growth of science and technology museums is characterized by a number of notable milestones, including the founding of institutions such as the London Science Museum in 1857 and the Smithsonian's National Museum of American History in 1964. These establishments had the goals of collecting, preserving, and displaying objects that were representative of the scientific and technological accomplishments of their respective nations, as well as developing public awareness of the processes that drove invention and development.

The Practices of Curators and the Caretaking of Collections

Curators, scientists, and historians are often employed by science and technology museums. These individuals are tasked with the responsibility of maintaining, preserving, and providing context for the museum's many exhibits. It is common practice for curators to work closely with specialists in a variety of scientific domains to assure the correctness and applicability of the exhibitions. Research, documenting, and preservation efforts are all part of the curation process. These steps are used to ensure that the historical context and scientific importance of artifacts and objects are preserved.

The process of "collection curation" involves choosing objects and technology for a museum's collection that are congruent with the institution's raison d'être and the primary focus of its exhibitions. These relics include some of the earliest scientific instruments and industrial machinery, as well as some of the most cutting-edge technology and equipment used for space travel.

MUSEUMS AND GALLERIES

The curators' goal is to provide a comprehensive portrayal of scientific and technical developments, thereby assisting visitors in following the development of ideas, innovations, and discoveries that have contributed to the formation of the contemporary world.

Exhibition Areas and Associated Interpretive Procedures

The exhibition spaces found in science and technology museums are often mesmerizing, and they have the ability to immerse visitors into the center of scientific research and technological wonders. These areas are intended to pique the interest of visitors of any age, and they do so in a variety of ways, including state-of-the-art multimedia presentations, hands-on interactive exhibits, and immersive displays. Interpretative practices provide visitors with insights into the historical context, scientific principles, and real-world applications of the technologies and discoveries displayed in the exhibitions. Visitors can receive these insights by visiting the exhibits.

Visitors are provided with context and scientific explanations through the use of informational signage, labels, and audio guides, which enables them to comprehend difficult ideas and appreciate the significance of advances in scientific research and technology. In addition, the use of interactive technology, such as simulations of virtual reality and overlays of augmented reality, enables visitors to participate in experiments, simulations, and hands-on activities that make learning an entertaining and informative experience. This technology includes augmented reality overlays and virtual reality simulations.

Programs for Education, as well as Involvement in the Community

The mission of science and technology museums is to increase scientific literacy, comprehension of technological advancements, and a heightened respect for creativity and originality. The majority of their efforts are focused on educational programs and getting people involved in their communities. These programs frequently consist of seminars, lectures, outreach activities, and guided tours, and they are geared toward a wide variety of groups, including students and families as well as technology enthusiasts and researchers. These museums encourage people to connect with scientific ideas and technology advancements by cultivating an environment that values education and encourages engagement from visitors.

In addition, several museums of science and technology work in conjunction with educational institutions, universities, and businesses in the technology sector to deliver instructional resources, mentoring programs, and internship opportunities. These museums play an important part in the development of the next generation of researchers and businesspeople by providing opportunities for young scientists and innovators.

Fostering Creativity and Curiosity in the Scientific Community

Inspiring scientific curiosity and creativity is one of the most important purposes that science and technology museums strive to accomplish. These institutions invite visitors to discover the wonders of the natural world and the promise of human creativity by presenting breakthroughs in subjects such as physics, chemistry, biology, and engineering. In addition, the museums encourage visitors to pursue professions in science and technology by showcasing the accomplishments of scientists, pioneers in technology, and other innovators in the field. This helps to stimulate both innovation and growth in the respective fields.

Keeping the Traditions of Technology Alive

Museums devoted to science and technology are essential to the conservation of technological history because they protect historical objects and innovations. These institutions ensure that technological developments from the past will not be forgotten and will continue to be available for future generations by engaging in practices of conservation and initiating archive efforts. In addition, the collections of science and technology museums frequently contain examples of technologies that are no longer in use because they have been superseded by more recent advances. These artifacts provide insights on the rapid pace of technological progress and the impact such changes have had on society.

Increasing People's Awareness of Ethical Considerations While Also Promoting Technological Literacy

Technology is advancing at a breakneck speed, and science and technology museums are playing an increasingly important part in fostering technological literacy and fostering ethical issues. They investigate the social consequences of developing technologies, discuss ethical conundrums, and offer chances for visitors to reflect on the influence that technology has had on both their lives and the society at large. These museums contribute to informed decision-making and ethical innovation by stimulating conversations about the responsible use of technology as well as the ethical implications of scientific and technological progress.

Science and technology museums are more than just archives of past scientific and technological accomplishments; they are also dynamic instructional places that celebrate the wondrous aspects of innovation, exploration, and discovery. These institutions excite scientific curiosity, encourage innovation, and improve our awareness of the ever-evolving world of science and technology through their curatorial methods, educational programs, and community engagement activities. Science and technology museums continue to define the narrative of scientific development and the tremendous impact it has on society. In their roles as guardians of technological history and drivers of technological literacy, these museums play an important role.

2.4 History and cultural heritage museums

The rich fabric of human history, customs, and cultural heritage is preserved and presented in museums of history and cultural heritage, which serve as stewards of the past and act as keepers of the past. These organizations are the custodians of cultural relics, documents, and artistic expressions that shed light on the social, political, and economic conditions as well as the cultural practices of a variety of various eras and geographic locations. History and cultural heritage museums cultivate a profound

MUSEUMS AND GALLERIES

understanding for the complexities of human civilization by means of interactive exhibits, educational activities, and interaction with the local community. These museums also inspire present and future generations to establish a connection with their ancestry.

The Development of Museums of History and Cultural Heritage throughout History

It is possible to trace the roots of history and cultural heritage museums all the way back to ancient civilizations, where royal collections, libraries, and archives functioned as repositories of cultural riches, historical records, and religious relics. These early civilizations laid the groundwork for the modern concept of history and cultural heritage museums. Nevertheless, the contemporary concept of public history museums evolved during the Enlightenment era in Europe. This development was spurred by the need to carefully catalog, preserve, and exhibit cultural artifacts and historical documents for the sake of public education and enjoyment.

Significant turning points in the evolution of public history and cultural heritage museums were

marked by the founding of organizations such as the British Museum in 1753 and the Louvre Museum in 1793, respectively. The goal of these establishments was to collect, conserve, and exhibit objects and works of art that represented the achievements of a variety of civilizations and cultures, all while developing an awareness of the societies, political systems, and artistic expressions that affected the course of human history.

The Practices of Curators and the Caretaking of Collections

Museums of history and cultural heritage often have curators, historians, and archaeologists on staff who are tasked with the responsibility of maintaining, preserving, and providing context for their respective holdings. The research, documenting, and conservation efforts that are a part of curatorial practices are extremely thorough and are designed to preserve the historical context, artistic integrity, and cultural relevance of the artifacts and artworks that are under their care.

Collection curation requires the employment of strategic acquisition tactics, in which curators pick artifacts and works of art with great care to ensure that they are in line with the goal of the museum and its primary thematic concern.

These picks ensure that the museum's collection is a wide and comprehensive representation of human history, artistic expressions, and cultural traditions by taking into account factors such as historical significance, cultural relevance, artistic merit, and educational value. In other words, these factors help ensure that the museum's collection is a good reflection of humanity.

Exhibition Areas and Associated Interpretive Procedures

The exhibition rooms available at history and cultural heritage museums are designed to be as immersive as possible in order to fully immerse visitors in the stories and narratives of the past. These areas have been thoughtfully crafted in order to provide visitors with a realistic and life-changing experience. This can be accomplished through the use of life-sized dioramas depicting historical scenes, interactive exhibits, or multimedia presentations. Interpretative techniques allow visitors to get insights into the historical context, social significance, and cultural relevance of the artifacts and artworks included in the exhibitions. These insights can be gained through the use of interpretative methods.

The visitor's knowledge of the exhibited goods is enhanced by the provision of context and explanations through the use of informational signage, labels, audio guides, and multimedia displays. Museums are now able to provide visitors with an engaging and engaging approach to learn about historical eras, cultural practices, and artistic trends by utilizing technology such as virtual reality experiences and augmented reality overlays.

Programs for Education, as well as Involvement in the Community

Museums of history and cultural heritage are committed to encouraging cultural awareness, historical comprehension, and a connection with one's background among their visitors. Educational programs and activities that encourage community engagement are extremely important factors in the realization of these goals. These programs frequently consist of guided tours, talks, seminars, and other types of outreach activities that are geared for a wide range of audiences, including students, families, cultural lovers, and scholars. History and cultural heritage museums develop a sense of cultural identity as well as a more profound understanding of the past by fostering an environment that values learning and participation as essential values.

In addition, many of these museums work together with local communities, educational institutions, and cultural organizations to provide instructional resources, share knowledge, and celebrate cultural traditions. They contribute to the maintenance of cultural heritage and help to build a sense of belonging among members of a variety of different cultural and ethnic groups through these actions.

Increasing Awarenes of Different Cultures And Connections Between Them

Museums of history and cultural heritage are important institutions because they provide a platform for fostering cultural knowledge and connectivity. These institutions celebrate the diversity of human civilizations and promote an understanding between people of diverse backgrounds by displaying objects and works of art that come from a variety of locations and time periods. They highlight the commonalities that bind us together and bring attention to the importance of cultural exchange and respect for one another.

Additionally, history and cultural heritage museums regularly participate in joint efforts with foreign institutions and organizations to foster cultural diplomacy and conversation. They do this by organizing cultural exchange programs and traveling exhibitions, which allows for the sharing of cultural experiences, traditions, and artistic expressions that transcends geographical barriers and cultivates a better appreciation for the cultural legacy of the world.

The protection of our identities and cultural heritage

The protection of cultural heritage and identity is one of the most important responsibilities that museums of history and cultural heritage have. These establishments assure the durability and authenticity of their collections by implementing stringent archival techniques and conservation procedures. This protects the collections from the effects of deterioration caused by the natural environment as well as the passage of time. By doing so, they play an essential part in the process of maintaining the cultural identities of a wide range of communities and ensuring that cultural legacy will continue to be available to future generations.

Providing Motivation for Future Generations While Also Promoting Cultural Stewardship

Museums of history and cultural heritage motivate succeeding generations to take up the mantle of cultural stewardship, which is essential to the ongoing protection of cultural heritage and the cultivation of an appreciation for historical narratives. They do this by encouraging young people to connect with their cultural roots, understand the traditions of their ancestors, and celebrate the beauty and complexity of human history and the various cultural expressions. This is done through educational programs, exhibitions, and involvement with the local community.

Museums of history and cultural heritage serve as pillars of cultural preservation, education, and enrichment. They contribute to a greater awareness of human history, artistic manifestations, and cultural traditions among the general public. These institutions continue to inspire and educate audiences through their curatorial methods, educational programs, and community participation, thereby establishing a deeper link with the past and the cultural richness that constitutes human civilization. As the custodians of history and cultural heritage, history and cultural heritage museums are tasked with ensuring that the legacies of our many distinct cultures and the historical narratives they tell will continue to be accessible and relevant for future generations.

2.5 Specialized and unique museums

Specialized and unique museums are institutions that cater to specialized interests, particular topics, or uncommon fields of study. These museums are engaging and distinctive in their own right. These museums go beyond the typical categories of art, history, or natural history and provide visitors with the opportunity to explore specialized knowledge, immerse themselves in one-of-a-kind experiences, and go deep into topics of interest that may not be widely known but are intensely fascinating nonetheless. During this in-depth investigation, we will investigate a wide range of specialized and one-of-a-kind museums, highlighting the outstanding qualities, curatorial methods, and contributions to education and cultural enrichment that each type of museum possesses.

1. **The Museo Subacuático de Arte (MUSA), which translates to "Underwater Art Museum"**

The MUSA Museum is a one-of-a-kind attraction that can be found in Cancun, Mexico. It is situated below the waters of the Caribbean Sea. It is the first underwater museum of art in the world and displays a collection of over 500 sculptures that have been submerged in the azure waters of the Mexican Caribbean. These sculptures are built from materials that are intended to encourage the growth of coral, which results in the creation of an artificial reef. Additionally, they provide an excellent backdrop for snorkelers, scuba divers, and people doing glass-bottom boat tours. MUSA is a prime example of how art and environmental protection may be intertwined to produce a one-of-a-kind and immersive experience for visitors. The museum serves in this capacity as an excellent example. The museum emphasizes the significance of protecting marine life and brings attention to the precarious condition of our seas in an effort to promote awareness.

2. **The Museum of Bad Art (MOBA): Honoring the Craft of Being Terrible at Art**

    The mission of the Museum of Bad Art (MOBA), which has locations in both Massachusetts and Ohio, is to acquire, preserve, and celebrate art that is "too awful to be ignored." It is a one-of-a-kind establishment that offers a venue for the exhibition of works of art that have been rejected by other museums or deemed insufficiently impressive in accordance with conventional criteria for artistic merit. MOBA provides a reviving and amusing perspective on the world of art by highlighting the fact that art can be interpreted in a variety of ways and demonstrating that even the most unorthodox or "bad" art has a place in the larger cultural conversation. The museum is dedicated to honoring the creative process and challenges visitors to reevaluate their preconceived conceptions of what constitutes artistic excellence and value.

3. **"Exploring the World of Hidden Animals" at the International Cryptozoology Museum**

    The International Cryptozoology Museum may be found in Portland, Maine, and is devoted to the investigation and discovery of cryptids. Cryptids are defined as creatures whose existence is not yet acknowledged by mainstream scientific research.

    The museum features a collection of exhibits, relics, and information pertaining to legendary creatures such as Bigfoot, the Loch Ness Monster, and the Chupacabra, in addition to less well-known cryptids from many cultures all over the world. The museum acts as a gathering place for people who are interested in the mysteries of the natural world, including cryptozoologists, enthusiasts, and curious visitors. It fosters a respect for the history and mythology that surrounds these elusive creatures while encouraging critical thinking and scientific investigation.

4. **A Curiosity Cabinet Filled with Unusual Exhibits Can Be Found Within the Museum of Jurassic Technology**

   The Museum of Jurassic Technology is an extraordinary establishment that blurs the barriers between fact and fantasy, art and science, and can be found in Los Angeles, California, in the United States. A wide variety of displays, ranging from historical items and scientific discoveries to creative installations and whimsical displays, are housed within the museum's extensive collection, which is known for its eclectic nature. It is well-known for the unique approach it takes to storytelling as well as its capacity to elicit interest and reflection in the minds of those who visit it. Visitors are encouraged to examine their preconceived views about history, science, and the nature of knowledge itself while at the museum, which fosters a sense of wonder and intellectual curiosity.

5. **The Museum of Broken Relationships: An Emotional Journey of Human Connections [An Emotional Journey of Human Connections]**

   The Museum of Broken Relationships is a forward-thinking establishment that first opened its doors in Zagreb, Croatia, and has since expanded to many sites across the world. It displays personal items and tales connected to broken relationships that have been donated by museum visitors. The collection of the museum contains souvenirs, photographs, letters, and other things that carry sentimental significance and tell moving stories of love, loss, and heartache. The museum encourages visitors to have more compassion, understanding, and a sense of connection with one another by offering a forum in which the general public can discuss the emotional experiences they have had. It is a celebration of the perseverance and healing that can result from emotional obstacles, while also serving as a monument to the universal human experiences of love and loss.

6. **The Icelandic Phallological Museum, Home to a Remarkable Assortment of Male Reproductive Organs**

   The Icelandic Phallological Museum may be found in the capital city of Reykjavik on the island of Iceland. Its mission is to collect, examine, and exhibit phallic specimens from a variety of animal species. The penises of a wide variety of animals, including whales, seals, land mammals, and even humans, are some of the specimens that may be found in the collection of the museum.

   It is a one-of-a-kind educational institution that investigates the historical and cultural relevance, as well as the biological diversity, of reproductive organs found in a variety of animals. The museum supports free discussion about human sexuality and the natural world by encouraging visitors to examine the interconnections of biology, sexuality, and cultural taboos.

7. **The Sulabh International Museum of Toilets: A Historical Journey of Sanitation [A Historical Journey of Sanitation]**

The Sulabh International Museum of Toilets is located in New Delhi, India. Its mission is to educate visitors about the origins, development, and current state of sanitation and toilets around the world. The displays at the museum showcase a variety of distinct toilet designs, sanitation technology, and historical items linked to sanitation practices that have been used by humans throughout the course of human civilization's development. It sheds light on the cultural, sociological, and technological significance of toilets in the context of improving public health and hygiene as well as the sustainability of the natural environment. The museum encourages visitors to reflect on the global difficulties of sanitation and the importance of access to clean and safe toilet facilities for human well-being. This inspires visitors to think about the museum's mission.

Museums that are both specialized and one-of-a-kind provide visitors with a wide variety of experiences that are both diverse and intriguing. These museums cater to specific interests, unconventional topics, and unique facets of human culture and knowledge. These institutions provide a forum for the investigation of unorthodox ideas, the promotion of open discourse, and the advancement of a more profound comprehension of a wide range of topics and specialties. These museums encourage inquisitiveness, critical thinking, and a deeper awareness for the myriad elements of the human experience through the unique approaches that they take to the curation and exhibition of their collections. They serve as important cultural assets that contribute to the expansion of humankind's collective knowledge and the appreciation of the myriad ways in which people express their individuality and creativity.

2.6 Virtual museums and the digital era

The advent of the digital era heralded the arrival of a revolutionary wave of technical advancement, which is currently transforming the world of museums. A new facet of cultural heritage preservation, education, and accessibility has materialized as a direct result of the proliferation of virtual museums. By utilizing technology to produce immersive and interactive experiences that transcend the confines of physical venues, these online institutions are revolutionizing the way in which we engage with art, history, science, and culture. In the course of this in-depth investigation, we will delve into the realm of virtual museums, investigating their historical roots, curatorial methods, impact on education, and role in the process of democratizing access to cultural material.

1. **The Impact of the Digital Age on the Development of Museums**

    The advent of the digital era, which was heralded by the widespread use of personal computers, the internet, and other forms of cutting-edge technology, had a tremendous effect on practically every facet of society, including the manner in which we approach cultural heritage and institutions. Traditional museums, despite the fact that they are vital repository of art, history, and culture, have historically been constrained in terms of the amount of available physical space,

MUSEUMS AND GALLERIES

accessibility, and ability to preserve fragile treasures.

The development of digital technologies has made it possible to create virtual museums, which circumvent many of the constraints that physical museums have. Users are able to explore collections, exhibits, and interactive displays from the comfort of their own devices, regardless of their physical location, thanks to the advent of virtual museums, which are essentially digital reproductions of traditional museums. This shift toward digital practices has made new opportunities available for preserving cultural heritage, interacting with it, and sharing it with others.

2. **The Origins of Online Museums in Their Physical Form**

   The idea of "virtual museums" may be traced back to the 1990s, when the World Wide Web was still in its infant stages and in its formative years. Digitizing photographs and information about museum collections and exhibitions was the primary focus of early efforts to create online museum experiences. These early digital endeavors had the goal of providing a static approximation of the actual experience of visiting a museum in person.

   The online presence of the Louvre, which offered high-resolution photographs of some of the museum's most famous artworks, was one of the pioneering examples of early virtual museums. This event marked the beginning of a transition toward digitizing museum collections and making them available to audiences all around the world.

   Because of advancements in technology, virtual museums have progressed from being simple web pages into fully immersive and interactive settings. The development of more dynamic and interesting digital museum experiences was made possible thanks to cutting-edge technology such as three-dimensional modeling, augmented and virtual reality, and other emerging technologies.

3. **The Role of Curatorial Practices in Online Museums**

   The process of digitization entails transforming physical items and artworks into digital representations. This technique is also known as "digitization." This may contain photographs with a high resolution, scans in three dimensions, or digital recreations of historical sites.

   The preservation of cultural heritage is made possible by digitization, which also makes it available to audiences all over the world.

   The process of selecting and organizing digital content, such as artworks, artifacts, documents, and multimedia components, is known as content curation. Curators in virtual museums perform this task. They develop storylines and exhibitions based on a particular theme in order to lead visitors through the content of the digital museum.

   Interactivity is a powerful tool that virtual museums utilize to attract and keep the attention of visitors. Interactive 3D models, virtual tours, multimedia presentations, and chances for user-generated content or comments are some examples of what this can include. Visitors are able to have a more engaging and immersive experience thanks to the use of interactive elements.

Accessibility: Virtual museums place a high priority on accessibility by making certain that its digital content can be accessed by a diverse audience of users, including people who have various types of disabilities. This may include the provision of alternative text for images, the provision of compatibility with screen readers, and the design of user-friendly interfaces.

Invention: Virtual museums are constantly on the lookout for creative new ways to exhibit cultural heritage. For this purpose, it may be necessary to do research and development with cutting-edge technologies such as augmented reality (AR) and virtual reality (VR) in order to produce one-of-a-kind and immersive experiences.

4. **Implications for Instruction and Education**

Access from Anywhere in the World Virtual museums remove the constraints of location, making it possible for people from all over the world to explore the collections and displays of physical museums. This global access is especially helpful for students and teachers who might not have the opportunity to visit actual museums in person.

Enhanced Learning Tools Virtual museums provide learning experiences that are both interactive and rich in multimedia content. Students get the opportunity to interact with 3D models, investigate historical sites, and gain access to in-depth knowledge regarding artworks and artifacts. Learning is made more interesting and easier to remember with these tools.

Learning in Multiple Disciplines: One of the benefits of visiting a virtual museum is the multiple disciplines that can be explored. Students looking for resources to help them with their studies in history, art, science, or any other field can find them in virtual museums. This contributes to a more well-rounded comprehension of our cultural heritage.

Accessibility: Virtual museums are inclusive and accessible to a wide variety of learners, including individuals who have physical or mental impairments. Everyone should have access to and be able to benefit from the materials offered by virtual museums, and this can be accomplished through the utilization of assistive technologies such as screen readers.

Academic Research and Scholarship Virtual museums facilitate academic research and scholarship by making digital collections and historical documents readily available to users. This facilitates study. Without the need to physically go to different museum locations, academics are able to perform in-depth research and analysis.

5. **Expanding Public Participation in the Access to Cultural Heritage**

Removing Obstacles Virtual museums do away with the logistical, geographic, and monetary obstacles that prevent people from accessing cultural material.

Explore digital collections from the comfort of your own home, even if you don't have the funds to visit actual museums or fly to far-flung locales.

Virtual museums make a contribution to the conservation of fragile or endangered objects by eliminating the need for physical storage space. The need to physically handle and expose fragile things is reduced when digital reproductions and 3D scans are used instead. This helps protect the items.

Inclusion of a Wide variety of civilizations and Historical Periods Virtual museums have the ability to depict a diverse variety of civilizations and historical periods. They have the capacity to bring to the foreground aspects of cultural history that are less well recognized, thereby fostering an atmosphere that is inclusive and understanding of a variety of cultures.

Open Access: Many online museums make their collections and other materials available to visitors without charging a fee. This concept of open access enables a wider transmission of cultural material, which is to the advantage of academic scholars, teachers, and the general public.

People from all over the world are able to learn about one other's heritage through the usage of virtual museums, which helps to promote cultural exchange between people from different regions of the world. This sharing of knowledge and comprehension leads to the appreciation of global culture and the connectedness of people around the world.

6. **Obstacles and Things to Take Into Account**

   The digital divide means that not everyone can visit virtual museums since they do not all have access to the internet or the requisite technologies. This results in a digital gap, which might make it more difficult for people to access cultural material.

   Authenticity: It's possible that virtual representations won't be able to fully capture the same sensory experience as visiting a real museum. It can be difficult to create an environment that is identical to that of a museum in terms of both the genuineness of the exhibits and the atmosphere.

   Preservation and Data Security: In order to avoid having digital collections and data be lost as a result of technological advancements, cyberattacks, or data corruption, sufficient preservation and data security measures are required.

   Curation and Context: The provision of context and interpretation are two of the most important functions that virtual museum curators perform. A crucial factor to take into account is ensuring that the curation is accurate and meaningful.

   Engagement and Interactivity: If virtual museums want to keep the interest of its visitors, they will need to continue to innovate. The importance of interactive features, user experience design, and relevant content cannot be overstated.

   Accessibility and inclusivity: It is of the utmost importance to make certain

that the resources of the virtual museum can be accessed by all individuals, especially those who have physical impairments.
7. **Some Illustrations of Online Museums**
Google Arts & Culture: Google Arts & Culture is an online platform that partners with museums, galleries, and cultural institutions all around the world to provide access to high-resolution photos of artworks, virtual tours, and historical content. This is made possible by Google's partnership with these organizations.

Users are given the opportunity to peruse the collections of the Louvre, the British Museum, the MET, and a great number of other illustrious organizations.

Virtual Tour of the Smithsonian National Museum of Natural History The Smithsonian National Museum of Natural History provides a virtual tour that guests can utilize to explore the museum's exhibits, such as the Hall of Fossils, Hall of Human Origins, and the Hope Diamond.

The Museum of Modern Art (MoMA) Offers a Variety of Online Exhibitions The Museum of Modern Art (MoMA) offers a variety of online exhibitions that provide an in-depth investigation of modern and contemporary art. The artworks, videos, and curator talks that are featured in these exhibitions are all available to view.

The Online Galleries of the British Library The online galleries of the British Library provide access to an extensive collection of historical documents, manuscripts, maps, and prints. The history of science and illuminated manuscripts are just two of the many themes that are covered by these digital resources.

The Digital Public Library of America (DPLA) is a digital library that collects content from a

variety of sources, including libraries, museums, and archives located all throughout the United States. It makes a wide variety of resources, such as images, manuscripts, books, and works of art, available to users without charge.

8. **The Prospects for the Development of Online Museums**

Virtual Reality (VR) and Augmented Reality (AR): Virtual Reality (VR) and Augmented Reality (AR) technologies have the ability to give very immersive experiences in virtual museums. Exhibits might be explored in three dimensions, visitors may interact with virtual objects, and visitors could even work together with others in a shared virtual area.

Artificial Intelligence (AI): AI has the potential to be utilized in order to improve the level of engagement and personalization that is present in virtual museum experiences. Visitors to digital collections may receive information on demand from chatbots and virtual guides powered by AI. These tools may also assist visitors in navigating digital collections.

Content Obtained Through Crowdsourcing Virtual museums may increasingly include content obtained from the general population through crowdsourcing. The user experience could be improved by allowing users to submit their own personal narratives, interpretations, and digital artifacts.

Holographic Exhibits Holographic displays and technologies can be used to produce lifelike replicas of items and historical figures within virtual museums, giving visitors the impression that they are physically there. This can be accomplished through the usage of holographic exhibits.

3D Printing and Replicas: Virtual museums might give 3D-printable files of select items, enabling visitors to make physical replicas of things from the digital collection. This would be accomplished through the usage of replicas.

Global Collaborations It is anticipated that virtual museums will participate in an increased number of collaborations and partnerships with institutions located all over the world. This will make the exchange of digital collections and specialized knowledge easier.

Education Will Be Improved Because Virtual Museums Offer Tailored Content And Interactive Experiences That Support A Wide Range Of Learning Objectives, Virtual Museums Will Continue To Serve As Valuable Resources For Educators In The Future.

In the realms of cultural heritage, educational opportunities, and open access, virtual museums are a force that is both dynamic and revolutionary. People from all around the world are now able to explore the rich resources of art, history, science, and culture with an ease that was not previously imaginable because to the digital institutions that have made this possible. Virtual museums are transforming the way we interact with our shared heritage by harnessing technology. These museums are also breaking down geographical barriers and providing cutting-edge tools for learning and research.

Virtual museums will play an increasingly essential role in the maintenance of cultural heritage, the promotion of education, and the facilitation of cultural interchange as they continue to develop and expand their operations. Because of their capacity to democratize access to our common human history, they are valuable assets in a world that is continuously undergoing transformation. Virtual museums provide a digital portal to the treasures of the past as well as the creativity of the present, whether the focus of the museum is on ancient objects, iconic artworks, or cultural traditions that are less well known.

Chapter 3

Curating and Conservation

Curating and conservation are two essential parts of the museum and cultural heritage area that play an essential role in the preservation, interpretation, and presentation of the artistic, cultural, and historical treasures that are found all over the world. The act of selecting, arranging, and presenting artifacts and works of art in an exhibition space such as a museum or gallery is known as "curating." On the other hand, conservation refers to the process of taking care of, restoring, and preserving these artifacts in order to ensure that they will last for many years and that future generations will continue to enjoy them.

This all-encompassing investigation goes deeply into the spheres of curation and conservation, investigating their historical roots, methodology, and ethical considerations, as well as the vital role that they serve in preserving the authenticity of our cultural legacy.

1. **The Origins and Development of Curating and Conservation Throughout History**

   The evolution of museums and people's perspectives on art, culture, and heritage are inextricably related to the history of conservation and the curation of collections inside those institutions. These spheres have, over the course of several centuries, been subjected to substantial alterations, which are a reflection of developments in curatorial practices and conservation strategies.

   1.1. Early administration of the collection and curatorial work

   Curating and collection management can be traced all the way back to ancient civilizations, where the practices were first developed. For example, in Mesopotamia, royal collections of art and artifacts were curated to demonstrate the richness and authority of the kings of the region. In a similar fashion, the ancient Egyptian pharaohs collected enormous collections of priceless artifacts, such as mummies, jewelry, and other works of art.

The word "museum," which comes from the Greek word "mouseion," was first used in ancient Greece and Rome, where it was the basis for the idea of a museum. These early institutions were founded with the purpose of preserving art and artifacts and displaying them, frequently within a philosophical or educational framework.

The Renaissance saw a flourishing of private collections of art and curiosities, which eventually evolved into the forerunners of modern museums. The concept of the museum was significantly influenced by prominent collectors such as the Medici family of Florence and the Roman College of the Vatican, both of which played critical roles in the development of the museum.

1.2. The Beginning of Contemporary Museums

The 18th century saw the founding of several of the world's earliest public museums, such as the British Museum (which was established in 1753) and the Louvre (which was established as a public museum in 1793). This marked a dramatic movement in curating methods away from private collections and toward public venues, as the organizations' goals were to make art and culture available to the general public.

The growth of nationalism and colonialism in the 19th century led to a spike in the purchase of cultural items and artworks from all over the world. This trend continued into the 20th century. Additionally, during this time period, the first art-only museums were established, such as London's National Gallery (established in 1824) and Boston's Museum of Fine Arts (established in 1870). Both of these institutions were formed in the 19th century.

1.3. The Origination of Different Conservation Methods

The expansion of museum collections and an increased understanding of the need to protect cultural property both occurred in the 19th century, which is when the origins of current conservation procedures can be traced back to. Those who were early pioneers in the discipline, such as Gustav Friedrich Waagen and Sir Charles Eastlake, started the process of developing rules for the restoration and maintenance of artworks.

The idea of conservation as a profession advanced further in the early 20th century with the founding of institutions such as the Courtauld Institute of Art in London and the Straus Center for Conservation and Technical Studies at Harvard University's Fogg Museum. Both of these establishments are examples of how the concept of conservation advanced. These establishments were crucial in the education of conservators as well as the advancement of conservation's scientific and ethical foundations.

2. **The Crucial Function of Curation in Institutions Such as Museums and Galleries**

Curating is a multidimensional activity that comprises a range of tasks, including generating exhibition themes, interpreting artworks for the public, and maintaining collections. Some of these activities include selecting artworks and objects for show, developing exhibition themes, and managing collections. The experience of the visitors is shaped by the curators, and they are responsible for communicating the cultural, historical, and artistic significance of the objects that are on show.

2.1. The Process of Selecting Items and Developing Collections

The selection of works of art and artifacts to be housed in a museum's permanent collection is one of the key responsibilities of a curator. It is common practice for curators to collaborate with acquisition committees, donors, and other specialists in order to locate items that are compatible with the collection philosophy and mission of an institution.

Deaccessioning, often known as the removal of things from a collection, is sometimes a part of
the process of developing a collection. This procedure needs careful deliberation and respect to ethical norms in order to ensure that deaccessioned things are handled responsibly, whether through the sale of the item, the transfer of the item to another institution, or the disposal of the item.

2.2. The Creation and Development of Exhibitions

When it comes to the creation of exhibitions, curators play a vital role. They come up with the ideas and develop the exhibits in order to attract and inform visitors. The first step in this process is to pick the objects that will be used, followed by the organization of those elements into a meaningful sequence, and finally the creation of narratives that will provide context and interpretation.

Another significant component of the curation process is the exhibition's physical layout and presentation. Lighting, display cases, and wall text are some of the ways that curators and exhibition designers work together to devise layouts that improve the experience of viewing the show for visitors.

2.3. The Giving of Meaning and Instruction

The task of interpreting artworks and other things in order to make them understandable to a wide range of people is the responsibility of curators. Creating exhibition labels, audio guides, and educational materials that provide context, historical background, and information about the artist or culture is a necessary step in this process. Visitors are encouraged to have a more in-depth interaction with the artwork through the use of interpretation.

The development of educational programming is another important aspect of a curator's job. To help visitors gain a deeper appreciation for the museum's holdings, curators often host educational events such as lectures, workshops, and guided tours.

2.4. The practice of Conservation and Preserving

Curators have an important role in lobbying for the conservation and long-term maintenance of a museum's collection, even if conservators are the professionals that specialize in the physical preservation of artworks. They work in tandem with art conservators to solve concerns regarding the preservation of works of art, such as making judgments regarding restoration, cleaning, and environmental conditions in display areas.

2.5. Academic Study and Investigation

In order to broaden their knowledge and improve their understanding of the collection, curators frequently participate in research and scholarly activities. They might also work with other academics in their field to contribute to scholarly publications, present their research at conferences, and collaborate on projects. The interpretation and presentation of the museum's collection are both improved as a result of this scholarly study.

3. The Importance of Conservation Work in Institutions Such as Museums and Galleries

The preservation, repair, and ongoing maintenance of cultural heritage objects are the primary foci of conservation efforts in museums and galleries. The major objective is to make sure that artworks and artifacts last for a long time by protecting them so that future generations can enjoy them. The term "conservation" can refer to a wide range of pursuits and actions.

3.1. Inspection and Compilation of Records

The first step in the conservation process is often an in-depth assessment of the object's current state, which is then meticulously documented. Microscopy, X-rays, and ultraviolet light are just some of the diagnostic tools that conservators employ to investigate the composition of an artwork, as well as its structure and any prior attempts at restoration. This assessment provides conservators with the information they need to make educated judgments regarding the object's treatment and restoration.

Documentation is vital for recording changes in the condition of an artwork over time. Additionally, documentation gives a reference point for any future conservation work that may be performed.

3.2. Cleaning and the Treatment of Surfaces

The cleaning process is an essential part of the conservation process. The surface of artworks are susceptible to accumulating dust, pollution, and other pollutants, which can have a negative impact on both their appearance and condition. Conservators employ a wide variety of cleaning techniques and chemicals in order to remove surface pollutants without causing damage to the underlying components of the artwork.

The consolidation of peeling paint, the repair of tears or losses, and the reattachment of disconnected pieces are all included in surface treatment. The artwork will be stabilized by these measures, and any further deterioration will be stopped.

3.3. Conservation of Existing Structures

In addition to working on the surface of works of art, conservators may also address the works' underlying structural problems. In the case of paintings, this may require mending a torn canvas, strengthening supports that have become weaker, or fixing structural deformations. When it comes to sculptures, structural conservation may involve reattaching limbs that have become disconnected or strengthening fissures in the object.

3.4. The Practice of Preventive Conservation

The goal of preventative conservation is to reduce the likelihood that artworks and artifacts will be damaged in any way. This involves taking measures to manage environmental elements like temperature and humidity as well as light, all of which have the potential to inflict irreparable harm. Conservators collaborate with museum professionals to plan appropriate storage and exhibition settings for the collection, which helps to maintain the collection's continued integrity throughout time.

3.5. Research and Investigation Based on Science

Conservators frequently engage with scientists and researchers to achieve the common goal of gaining a more in-depth understanding of the components and processes that go into making artwork. The results of scientific study can help guide treatment decisions and guide conservators in their selection of the materials and methods that are best suited for restoration.

3.6. Both morality and deliberation are involved.

The process of decision-making for conservators is guided by a stringent ethical code, which they must adhere to. This code places a strong emphasis on transparency, honesty, and a commitment to the preservation of the historical and artistic significance of an artwork. The decisions on treatment and restoration are made after discussion with curators and other experts, as well as after a comprehensive examination and recording of the object in question.

3.7. Collaborating with the curators and the management of the collections

In order to guarantee that artworks are cared for and handled appropriately, conservators collaborate closely with museum curators and other members responsible for collections management. They contribute knowledge and skills about the preservation requirements of the collection, and they work together to design exhibitions and transfer objects.

4. Curating and Conservation: Ethical Considerations and Obstacles

The fields of curating and conservation in the museum and gallery world follow the same set of ethical principles in order to ensure the responsible care of cultural heritage. These principles were developed by the American Alliance of Museums (AAM). The specific issues that curators and conservators encounter can be helped in part by adhering to these guidelines.

4.1. Responsibility and Compensatory Payments

The questions of ownership and restitution provide one of the most significant ethical difficulties in the industry as a whole. The provenance of a museum's or gallery's collection is becoming an increasingly important topic of discussion, particularly in instances in which cultural artifacts were acquired through dubious means or during times of conflict or colonial authority. Curators and conservators have the responsibility of navigating these difficult concerns and working toward ethical solutions, which may include repatriation, loans, or collaborative shows.

4.2. Authenticity, as well as Restorative Measures
The problem of maintaining an artwork's authenticity while still performing any essential restoration work is one that never goes away. Curators and conservators have the responsibility of determining when and how an artwork should be restored, all the while keeping in mind that excessive restoration might reduce the historical and artistic worth of an object. In the process of rehabilitation, both ethical decision-making and transparency are absolutely necessary.

4.3. Ability to Participate and Accessibility
The public's access to museum and gallery collections is becoming an increasingly important priority for these institutions. It is the responsibility of curators and conservators to investigate ways in which cultural material might be made more accessible to a wider variety of audiences, including individuals with disabilities. This includes making the exhibit design, descriptions, and teaching materials accessible to those with disabilities.

4.4. Responsibility and Sustainability with Regards to the Environment
Concerns about the environment have emerged as an issue of paramount importance in the
field of cultural heritage. To lessen their impact on the surrounding environment, museums and galleries need to implement more sustainable policies and procedures. This includes the use of appropriate conservation treatments, the creation of environmentally friendly show designs, and the implementation of collection management procedures that place an emphasis on preserving the environment.

4.5. Developments in the State of Technology
It is important for curators and conservators to keep up with the latest technological developments in their area. Although new tools and methods for preservation and interpretation are made available by technological advancements, these advancements also present obstacles in terms of data security and compatibility over the long term. The application of technology raises a number of important moral and ethical questions.

5. Recent Developments in the Fields of Curating and Conservation
In recent years, new breakthroughs in the domains of curation and conservation have increased the capabilities and promise of both fields. The advancements in technology, the working together of specialists from many fields, and an

increasing focus on audience participation and education are the sources of these breakthroughs.

5.1. Curation of Digital Content

The importance of digital curation to curatorial methods has grown substantially in recent years.

It entails the arrangement and management of digital content, such as digitized collections, interactive displays, and multimedia presentations, among other types of digital media. Through the use of digital curation, it is now possible to construct virtual exhibitions that are open to audiences all over the world.

5.2. Both Augmented Reality (AR) and Virtual Reality (VR) are types of mixed reality.

The use of AR and VR technology is bringing about a sea change in the way that exhibitions are conceived of and experienced. Because of these technologies, visitors are able to interact with artworks and artifacts in ways that are both immersive and interactive, which results in a greater comprehension of the collection as a whole. Using augmented reality (AR) apps, for instance, guests have the ability to superimpose additional information, animations, or historical context onto a work of art.

5.3. The Science of Conservation

The precision and efficacy of conservation practices have both increased as a result of recent developments in the science of conservation. The possibilities for preserving cultural heritage have expanded as a result of the development of high-resolution imaging tools, non-invasive analysis methods, and creative materials for restoration.

5.4. Participation of the Public and Cooperative Efforts with the Community

Collaboration with local communities and active participation from the general public are becoming increasingly important to museums and galleries. In order to achieve this goal, it is necessary to work together with local communities, artists, and other stakeholders to develop exhibitions and programming that are reflective of a variety of perspectives and experiences.

In the museum space, the intention is to encourage a sense of ownership as well as inclusivity among visitors.

5.5. Online Access and 3D Tours are Available

The advent of the digital era has resulted in a shift in emphasis toward accessing information online and taking part in virtual tours. Virtual tours and user-friendly websites that let visitors examine museum collections from any location in the world are becoming increasingly common features among museums and art galleries as they work to grow their online presence. This digital outreach makes education and accessibility easier to achieve.

6. The Prospects for Curating and Conservation in the Future

6.1. Improved Participation in Digital Activities

The digital interaction with artworks and artifacts will become more complex as technology continues to improve. Augmented reality, virtual reality, and other forms of interactive technology will provide tourists with new avenues to investigate and comprehend the world's cultural legacy.

6.2. Cooperation Between Different Disciplines

There will be an increase in the number of instances in which distinct fields, such as art history, conservation science, and computer science, are brought together. The collaboration of experts from different fields will result in the development of novel techniques to study, curating, and conservation.

6.3. Cooperation on a Global Scale

The exchange of resources, assets, and professional knowledge will become increasingly commonplace among museums and galleries operating on a worldwide scale. Through their combined efforts, people from all around the world will be able to gain exposure to a larger range of cultural ideas.

6.4. Both Conservation and Long-Term Sustainability

The importance of a sustainable future will be maintained in conservation activities. There will be an increase in the use of sustainable technologies and environmentally conscious exhibition design in museums. The use of materials and techniques that have the smallest possible negative impact on the environment will be given priority throughout conservation efforts.

6.5. Experiences That Are Centered Around the Audience

The process of curation will place a larger emphasis on the creation of experiences that center on the audience. The goal of museums will be to pique the interest of visitors through curated exhibits, interactive programs, and initiatives pushed by the local community.

6.6. Considerations of an Ethical Nature

Ethical concerns will continue to play an important role in the curatorial and conservation activities that are carried out. The challenges of cultural sensitivity, accessibility, and provenance will continue to be addressed by museums and galleries.

The act of preserving and interpreting our cultural history relies heavily on curating as well as conservation, both of which are vital practices. Even if these professions have advanced a great deal over the course of the centuries, they are still absolutely necessary in order to make sure that artworks and artifacts are preserved and may be accessed. The dynamic character of the museum and gallery business is reflected in the issues that curators and conservators encounter in terms of ethics as well as the inventive developments that they pursue. The future of curating and conservation holds the promise of increased digital engagement, interdisciplinary collaboration, global outreach, and a continued commitment to ethical considerations and sustainable practices. All of these factors contribute to the responsible stewardship of our world's artistic, cultural, and historical treasures.

3.1 The role of curators in shaping museum collections

When it comes to the formation of museum collections, curators play a crucial part. They have a significant impact on the selection, organization, interpretation, and preservation of works of art, antiquities, and cultural objects. Curators are the storytellers and guardians of a museum's collection, ensuring that it reflects the institution's goal and fulfills the educational and cultural needs of its audience. Their responsibilities go beyond simply purchasing and showing works; instead, they are responsible for making sure that the collection does so. This essay examines the historical foundations, curatorial techniques, ethical considerations, and impact on cultural legacy of museum curators, delving into the varied role that curators play in the process of shaping museum collections and curating museum exhibits.

1. **The Origins of Museums and the Curatorial Profession**
   Both the activity of curating and the idea of museums may be traced back to significant points in human history. The origin of the word "museum" may be traced back to the Greek word "mouseion," which was used to refer to a location that encouraged education and the pursuit of knowledge. Curating and museums as we know them now have come a long way, but their roots may be found in a variety of different historical practices and institutions.

   1.1. The First Galleries, Museums, and Collections
   The practice of collecting and displaying artifacts extends back to the earliest known civilizations. The wealthy and powerful city-state rulers of Mesopotamia gathered vast collections of art and artifacts to display their riches and might. These collections included works of art as well as artifacts. In a similar manner, the pharaohs of ancient Egypt amassed vast art collections, extensive jewelry collections, and even mummies. The idea of a museum first began to take shape in ancient Greece and Rome. The Lyceum in Athens, which served as a center of learning and knowledge, was one of the earliest examples of this.

   During the Renaissance, the practice of collecting works of art and other oddities grew increasingly popular. This gave rise to the term "curator." Important sponsors, such as the Medici family in Florence and the Roman College of the Vatican, played critical roles in the process of assembling art and artifact collections.

   1.2 The Beginnings of Contemporary Museums
   The development of museums underwent a momentous transition somewhere during the 18th century. Moving away from the private and royal collections that were common in earlier centuries, establishments like the British Museum (which was formed in 1753) and the Louvre (which was created as a public museum in 1793) were among the first to make their collections accessible to the general public. These early public museums were founded with the intention of making art and culture available to a wider audience, so paving the way for the

development of the contemporary museum.

The rise of nationalism and colonialism in the 19th century resulted in the collecting of cultural items from all over the world. Additionally, this time period saw the construction of museums that were solely dedicated to art collections, such as the National Gallery in London (which was created in 1824) and the Museum of Fine Arts in Boston (which was formed in 1870). Both of these museums may be located in the United Kingdom.

2. **The Complexity of the Role Played by Curators**

Curators are responsible for the upkeep, interpretation, and education of the collections housed in museums. Their responsibilities include a wide variety of tasks that help in the acquisition, interpretation, and preservation of works of art and other cultural artifacts.

2.1. The Growth of the Collection and New Acquisitions

The expansion of existing collections is one of the key responsibilities of curators. Performing this duty requires selecting pieces of art and other items that will become part of the museum's collection.

To ensure that the selected works are in keeping with the goals and objectives of the organization, curators collaborate closely with acquisition committees, benefactors, and subject matter experts, and they frequently adhere to stringent standards or collection policies.

Deaccessioning, which is the process of removing things from a collection, is also included in the process of developing a collection. When it comes to deaccessioning artifacts, curators are tasked with making decisions that are both meticulous and ethical. These decisions may involve the sale of an item, its transfer to another institution, or its disposal.

2.2. The Development and Design of the Exhibition

The exhibition planning and design process is mostly driven by the work of the curators. They come up with the ideas and develop the exhibits in order to attract and inform visitors. This process involves selecting artifacts, putting them in a meaningful order, developing narratives that provide context and understanding, and deciding how the exhibits will be physically laid out.

In museum curation, collaborating with exhibition designers is a frequent practice. This is because the physical design of exhibitions is one of the most important factors in enhancing the experience of museum visitors. Together with designers, curators develop exhibition layouts that make the best use of lighting, display cases, wall text, and other components that add to the exhibition's overarching aesthetic and narrative.

2.3. Explanation and Instruction

The task of interpreting works of art and other artifacts in a manner that makes them understandable to a wide range of people is the responsibility of curators. They produce exhibition labels, audio guides, and other educational materials that offer context, historical background, and information about the artist or culture in question. Interpretation is an essential component of museum curation because it inspires visitors to have a more in-depth interaction with the works of art on display.

Curators also play a significant role in the creation of educational programming. They may host talks, workshops, and guided tours in order to deepen the visitor's experience and improve their comprehension of the collections. This will allow for a more engaging and interactive environment.

2.4. The Practice of Conservation and Preserving

Curators are responsible for the overall conservation and long-term maintenance of a museum's collection, whereas conservators are experts in the physical preservation of artworks.

They work in tandem with art conservators to solve concerns regarding the preservation of works of art, such as making judgments regarding restoration, cleaning, and environmental conditions in display areas.

2.5. Research and Academic Achievement

In order to broaden their knowledge and improve their understanding of the collection, curators frequently participate in research and scholarly activities. They might also work with other academics in their field to contribute to scholarly publications, present their research at conferences, and collaborate on projects. The interpretation and presentation of the museum's collection are both improved as a result of this scholarly study.

3. The Curating Process and Its Ethical Considerations

When it comes to curating techniques, ethical issues are of the utmost importance. In order to ensure the preservation of cultural assets in a responsible manner, curators are required to abide by a set of ethical norms. These principles address concerns with acquisition, deaccessioning, authenticity, and provenance, among other relevant topics.

3.1. Origin and Statement of Ownership

An important factor to take into account is an item's provenance, also known as its previous owners and their relationships. The curators are responsible for conducting a thorough investigation of the collection's history to ascertain whether or not the items were obtained in an honest and moral manner. When there is uncertainty regarding the origin of an item, additional investigation and careful attention to detail are necessary steps to take.

3.2. Authenticity and Responsibility for the Work

It is a continuing effort to find a happy medium between the requirements of investigation and verification and the need to protect the authenticity of an artwork. The curator is responsible for deciding when and how to authenticate an artwork, as well as whether or not to conduct research on the artwork's origin or conduct attribution studies. It is a delicate responsibility to answer any suspicions regarding the authenticity of an artwork while also preserving the quality of the artwork itself.

3.3. Sensitivity to Different Cultures and Repatriation

In the most recent few years, concerns regarding cultural sensitivity and repatriation have garnered a substantial amount of attention. When it comes to objects that were obtained by means that could be construed as unethical or unlawful, curators have a responsibility to be aware of the issues that pertain to cultural heritage and to strive toward finding fair and ethical solutions, including repatriation.

3.4. Availability of Access and Inclusion

There has been a recent uptick in efforts by museums to broaden the audience base that can experience their exhibits. It is the responsibility of curators to identify ways in which cultural material might be made more accessible to a wider range of audiences, including individuals with disabilities. This includes making the exhibit design, descriptions, and teaching materials accessible to those with disabilities.

3.5. Integrity and Openness in the Process of Interpretation

The curator is accountable for providing a clear and morally sound interpretation of the works of art and artifacts in their care. They are obligated to present information and narratives that are true to history, respectful to cultures, and unbiased. The audience is ensured to obtain a comprehensive and correct comprehension of the collection through the use of ethical interpretation.

4. The Role of Curators in the Preservation of Cultural Heritage

The work of curators has a significant bearing on the function that cultural heritage plays in society. Their work has an impact on the ability to maintain cultural items and make them accessible to the public, as well as on the education of the general public and the comprehension of history, art, and culture. The following are some of the ways curators are responsible for shaping cultural heritage:

4.1 The Safeguarding of Our Cultural Heritage

Curators play an important role in the protection of cultural heritage by using their expertise to make judgments regarding the purchase, maintenance, and preservation of artworks and other objects. Because of their work to advocate for the collection's continued preservation over the long term, cultural heritage will be around for future generations to enjoy.

4.2. Educational Programming and Explanatory Materials

Curators contribute to the educational goals of museums by developing exhibitions and modes of interpretation that make the nation's cultural legacy more approachable and interesting to visitors. They enhance the visitor's comprehension of the collection by providing context, historical narratives, and information about the items in the collection.

4.3. Participation of the Audience

It is the job of curators to devise exhibitions and programs that will captivate and motivate visitors. Their responsibilities do not consist solely of selecting and presenting artifacts; rather, they must also think about how to pique the interest of the audience and produce an experience that will be unforgettable.

4.4. Intercultural Communication and Discussion

Museums and other cultural organizations play an important part in promoting cultural interaction and conversation. The curators choose objects to put on exhibit that reflect a variety of cultures and historical periods to promote a deeper comprehension of the cultural diversity that exists throughout the world.

4.5. Contribution to the Academic Community

Curators make important contributions to the academic world by conducting original research, publishing their findings, and working closely with other scholars and industry professionals. The academic community is informed and their knowledge of cultural heritage is expanded as a result of their efforts.

5. Developments in the Methods of Curatorial Work

The selection, presentation, and interpretation of museum collections have all improved as a result of new innovations and technology, which have been incorporated into curatorial practices over time. These advancements have completely changed the museum curation industry and have opened up a wealth of intriguing opportunities for the future:

5.1. Curation of Digital Content

The importance of digital curation to curatorial methods has grown substantially in recent years. It entails the management of digital content, such as digitized collections, multimedia presentations, and interactive displays, among other types of digital media. The production of virtual exhibitions that are open to audiences all over the world is made possible by digital curation.

5.2. Augmented Reality (AR) and Virtual Reality (VR) are both types of mixed reality.

The use of augmented and virtual reality technologies is causing a shift in how exhibitions are conceived of and experienced. By allowing visitors to connect with artworks and objects in more immersive and interactive ways, these technologies open up new possibilities for visitors to gain a deeper understanding of the collection.

5.3. Collaborative Efforts Between Disciplines

Collaboration between curators and specialists from a wide variety of fields, including as art history, conservation science, and computer science, is becoming increasingly common. The collaboration of experts from different fields results in novel ways to research, exhibition curation, and interpretation.

5.4. Inclusivity and Collaborative Work with the Community

Museums and other cultural institutions are placing a greater emphasis on inclusiveness and community partnerships. Exhibitions and programs that are reflective of a variety of perspectives and experiences are being developed by curators in collaboration with local communities, artists, and other partners. This strategy helps to instill a sense of ownership and belonging among visitors to the museum's space.

5.5. Online Access and Virtual Tours

The advent of the digital era has resulted in a shift in emphasis toward accessing information online and taking part in virtual tours. Virtual tours and user-friendly websites that let visitors study museum exhibits from any location in the world are becoming increasingly common features among museums as they work to grow their online presence. This digital outreach makes education and accessibility easier to achieve.

6. The Prospects for Museum Curation and the Preservation of Cultural Heritage

6.1. Improved Participation in Digital Activities

The digital interaction with works of art and other items will become more nuanced and sophisticated as technological advancements continue. Augmented reality, virtual reality, and other forms of interactive technology will provide tourists with new avenues to investigate and comprehend the world's cultural legacy.

6.2. Collaborative Efforts Between Disciplines

There will be an increase in the number of instances in which distinct fields, such as art history, conservation science, and computer science, are brought together. The collaboration of experts from different fields will result in novel ways to research, museum curation, and cultural interpretation.

6.3. Cooperation on a Global Scale

The exchange of resources, assets, and professional knowledge will become increasingly commonplace among museums operating on a global scale. Through their combined efforts, people from all around the world will be able to gain exposure to a larger range of cultural ideas.

6.4. Long-Term Viability and Protecting the Environment

The importance of a sustainable future will be maintained in conservation activities. There will be an increase in the use of sustainable technologies and environmentally conscious exhibition design in museums. The use of materials and techniques that have the smallest possible negative impact on the environment will be given priority throughout conservation efforts.

6.5. Experiences That Are Centered On The Audience

The process of curation will place a larger emphasis on the creation of experiences that center on the audience. The goal of museums will be to pique the interest of visitors through curated exhibits, interactive programs, and initiatives pushed by the local community.

The central and complex function that curators play in the formation of museum collections is essential. They have an impact on the selection of artworks, items, and cultural heritage; how these things are interpreted; how they are preserved; and how they are presented. Curators are stewards of cultural legacy, and as such, they are responsible for making collections accessible, inclusive, and engaging. They are also influenced in their work by ethical considerations. Curators have an influence that may be felt well beyond the four walls of a museum; this impact can be seen in the areas of the preservation of cultural heritage, teaching, audience engagement, cultural exchange, and scholarly research. Innovations in digital engagement, interdisciplinary collaboration, global outreach, sustainability, and audience-centered experiences are altering the way museums connect with their audiences and serve the cultural and educational requirements of society. The future of curation holds promise. For the foreseeable future, curators will continue to play an essential part in preserving and shaping the cultural legacy of people all over the world.

3.2 Conservation and preservation of artifacts

The preservation and conservation of antiquities, works of art, and other cultural items are essential activities that preserve their durability and maintain their original integrity. These processes encompass a variety of actions and methods that are aimed to protect these artifacts from degradation and destruction so that they can be enjoyed and studied by future generations. This will allow for them to be preserved for longer. In this section, we will have a cursory discussion on the fundamental ideas and procedures that are involved in the conservation and preservation of artifacts.

1. **The Inquiry and the Accumulation of Evidence**

   The first step in the process of conserving and preserving an artifact is typically an in-depth analysis and documenting of the object's current state. This step is necessary in order to gain a grasp of the object's components, its structure, and any problems that may exist that require care. For more in-depth examination, more sophisticated instruments such as microscopes, ultraviolet light, and X-rays may be utilized.

   Conservators are better able to make educated decisions on the treatment and restoration of an item when they have access to accurate documentation.

2. **Sanitation and the Treatment of Surfaces**

   The act of cleaning is essential to the processes of conservation and preservation. Over time, dust, grime, pollutants, and other types of surface contaminants can build up on artifacts, which can have a negative impact on both their appearance and their condition. Conservators employ a wide variety of cleaning strategies and chemicals in order to remove these impurities without causing any damage to the materials that lie beneath the surface.

   The consolidation of peeling paint, the repair of tears or losses, and the reattachment of disconnected pieces are all included in surface treatment. The objective of these operations is to maintain the artifact's stability and forestall any further deterioration.

3. **Preserving the Building's Structure**
It's possible that artifacts need to have their structures conserved in order to fix the problems with their physical integrity. For instance, paintings may experience damage in the form of tears or deformations, whereas sculptures may suffer damage to the supports that hold them up or the detachment of limbs. Conservators will seek to fix and stabilize these structural concerns in order to ensure the artifact will remain stable over the long term.

4. **Preventive and Environmental Conservation**
The goal of preventative conservation is to reduce the number of potential threats to artifacts. This involves taking measures to regulate environmental conditions such as temperature, humidity, and light exposure, all of which have the potential to cause irreparable harm. Conservators and staff members in charge of managing collections collaborate in order to devise storage and exhibition conditions that are suitable for the item and will assure its continued integrity throughout time.

5. **Analyses and Investigations in the Field of Science**
Conservators frequently work together with scientists and other researchers to obtain a more in-depth understanding of an artifact's construction methods and materials. The results of scientific study are used to influence treatment decisions and to assist conservators in selecting the materials and methods that will be most effective for restoration. Methods such as spectroscopy, radiography, and microscopic analysis could be utilized here.

6. **Morality and Determination of Actions**

In their line of work, conservators are expected to abide by a rigorous code of ethics that places an emphasis on openness, honesty, and a dedication to the protection of an artifact's historical and artistic significance. The decisions on treatment and restoration are made after discussion with curators and other experts, as well as after a comprehensive examination and recording of the object in question.

3.3 Ethical dilemmas in museum curation

The curation of museums is a complicated topic that incorporates a wide variety of moral and ethical considerations. As a result, curators are frequently required to make difficult choices that strike a balance between the preservation and interpretation of cultural legacy and ethical, moral, and legal issues. These conundrums may have their origins deep inside concerns such as provenance, cultural sensitivity, repatriation, accessibility, and the confluence of political context and cultural context. In this section, we will investigate some of the most important ethical conundrums that curators have to deal with in order to appropriately oversee the care of museum collections.

1. **Origin and Statement of Ownership**
   The question of who originally owned an artifact or piece of artwork is one of the most significant ethical conundrums that arises in the process of museum curation. The history of an object must be thoroughly researched by curators, as they are responsible for ensuring that it was obtained in a moral and lawful manner. The difficulty comes whenever there is uncertainty regarding the origin of an item, as well as if there are allegations of theft or looting. The curators are responsible for navigating these difficult issues and making well-informed decisions regarding whether or not to keep, repatriate, or negotiate with claimants.
2. **Return to Country**
   The question of whether or not cultural relics should be returned to their original locations is one that is ethically fraught and highly contentious. Many museums worldwide house relics obtained during periods of colonization or under circumstances that some believe to be unethical or criminal. When there are compelling justifications for repatriation based on the relevance of the object to its country of origin, such as its historical or cultural significance, curators are frequently put in the difficult position of deciding whether or not to return the piece to its country of origin.
3. **Cultural Sensitivity**
   When exhibiting artifacts, museums make an effort to be culturally sensitive and to include people of various backgrounds. However, curators are tasked with striking a fine balance between educating the general public about many cultures and respecting the beliefs, values, and traditions of those nations. This may be a challenging task. The wrong interpretation or portrayal of an object might result in ethical conundrums and worries about cultural appropriation.
4. **Availability of Access**
   Museums are progressively working to make their collections accessible to various audiences, including those with impairments. The curators of a collection are faced with the moral conundrum of how to make the collection accessible to the public without jeopardizing its safety or its ability to be preserved. It can be a difficult job to design exhibits and explanation that are inclusive of all visitors while still safeguarding the items on display.
5. **Historical, Social, and Political Context**
   The historical, political, and cultural significance of the items in a museum's collection can often present difficult moral choices. Objects that were first obtained without any sort of controversy may, at a later time, become contentious topics of discussion as a result of shifting political landscapes or developing cultural sensitivities. The effects of these altering contexts on the presentation and understanding of objects are something that curators need to take into consideration.
6. **The Importance of Ethics and Transparency in Interpretation**

Furthermore, ethical considerations should be taken into account while interpreting artifacts. The information and narratives that curators present to the public must be free of bias, while also being historically accurate and culturally sensitive. The difficulty lies in presenting information in a way that accurately portrays the complication and diversity of the topic at hand while preserving objectivity and showing respect for the various points of view.

Curators have a challenging and never-ending uphill battle to successfully navigate these difficult ethical conundrums. Their job is to make decisions that are well thought out, accountable, and open to public scrutiny. These choices should put the protection of museum collections and the educational value of their exhibits at the forefront, while also taking into account and addressing ethical, moral, and legal considerations. These problems underline the dynamic and growing nature of the museum field and the continual commitment of curators to the responsible conservation of cultural property.

Chapter 4

Museums as Educational Institutions

Since the beginning of time, people have looked up to museums as trusted custodians of art, history, and cultural traditions. In addition to their function as storage locations for priceless artifacts, museums also play an important role as influential educational organizations. Learning may be transformed into an immersive and pleasurable experience thanks to the exceptional capacity of museums to captivate, instruct, and inspire visitors. We dig into the multifaceted world of museums as educational institutions, their historical evolution, their significance in current culture, their instructional practices, and the growing role that they are playing in creating the future of education in this all-encompassing investigation.

1. **The opening statement**
   It is common practice to consider museums to be the keepers of our collective cultural, historical, and artistic history. Because of this, museums occupy a special and valued role in society. Nevertheless, their function goes beyond merely that of preservation and curation. The role of museums as influential educational institutions that make important contributions to both formal and informal education has grown dramatically throughout the years.
   In the course of this in-depth investigation, we shall investigate the myriad of facets that museums as educational institutions possess. We are going to investigate the historical history of museums, the many different types of museums, the educational methods museums utilize, as well as the significance of museums in today's society. In addition, we will talk about the impact that they have had on both official and informal education as well as the potential that they have to alter the future of learning.
2. **The Evolution of Museums Into Leading Educational Institutions Throughout History**
   2.1 The Age of Enlightenment and the Beginning of the Public Museum

MUSEUMS AND GALLERIES

Movement

The Age of Enlightenment, which occurred in Europe during the 17th and 18th centuries, was a critical period in the evolution of museums into educational institutions. Reason, knowledge, and the importance of education were highly valued by philosophers of the Enlightenment period. Because of this, public museums came into being, providing a wider audience with access to art, culture, and other forms of information.

Examples of this change include the British Museum, which was established in 1753, and the Louvre, which first opened its doors to the public in 1793, during the French Revolution. A break from the private collections owned by monarchs, nobles, and religious organizations, these institutions signaled the beginning of a new era.

2.2. The Evolution of Educational Practices During the 19th Century

In the 19th century, a proliferation of museums devoted to various subjects, including art, science, history, and others, came into being. In addition, educational reforms that advocated for the use of museum materials into formal education were implemented during this time period. Not only were museums transformed into destinations for leisure, but they also evolved into significant resources for academic institutions and teachers.

3. Different Categories of Museums that Function as Educational Institutions

3.1. Art Galleries and Museums

The Metropolitan Museum of Art in New York and the Louvre in Paris are two examples of art museums that provide visitors with a comprehensive educational experience that is centered on visual arts. They give spectators the opportunity to connect with a wide variety of artistic traditions, styles, and techniques. Art museums frequently offer educational programs, exhibitions, and resources aimed not only at the general public but also at more specialized groups.

3.2. Natural Science Galleries and Museums

Visitors can learn about the natural world at natural history museums such as the American Museum of Natural History in New York or the Natural History Museum in London. These establishments maintain extensive collections of biological specimens, fossils, minerals, and anthropological items in their archives and storage facilities. They provide instructional programs that center on topics such as evolution, biodiversity, and the history of the earth.

3.3. Museums Devoted to Science and Technology

Hands-on educational opportunities may be found at science and technology museums all over the world, including the Museum of Science and Industry in Chicago and the Deutsches Museum in Munich, to name just two examples.

They do this by providing visitors with interactive displays that investigate scientific ideas, technological advancements, and the influence science has on people's everyday lives.

3.4. Museums of Past Civilizations and Cultural Heritage

History museums, such as the Smithsonian National Museum of American History in Washington, D.C., and cultural heritage museums, such as the British Museum, display the historical and cultural wealth of their respective societies. The museums display artifacts, records, and exhibitions that convey the stories of human civilization. As a result, visitors are able to get a more in-depth comprehension of both their own history and the variety of civilizations found across the world.

3.5. Museums That Are Both Unique And Specialized

There are museums that are dedicated to particular subjects or areas of interest. For instance, the International Spy Museum in Washington, District of Columbia, digs into the realm of espionage and provides educational insights into the history of intelligence, as well as security and safety. In a similar vein, unusual museums, such as the Museum of Bad Art in Massachusetts, cultivate unorthodox educational experiences that question standard conceptions of art and culture.

3.6. Online Galleries and the Emergence of the Digital Age

The rise of the internet has led to the establishment of "virtual museums," which may be visited via the internet. These institutions provide virtual tours, interactive displays, and digital resources, making it possible for audiences all over the world to experience collections without having to leave the comfort of their own homes. The nature of educational institutions is changing in this day and age, and one example of this is the rise of virtual museums.

4. Educational Methodologies Employed in Museums

4.1. Exhibits With Interpretive Text

Visitors are kept interested by the use of storytelling, interactive displays, and multimedia components in interpretive exhibits. They enhance the visitor's comprehension of the collection by providing context, historical narratives, and information about the items in the collection.

4.2. Activities That Involve Your Hands

Experience-based education is emphasized through the use of hands-on activities in numerous museums. Visitors have the opportunity to touch, experiment, and create, all of which contribute to an enhanced understanding of complicated subjects.

4.3. Educational Programs and Workshops

Museums typically provide a diverse selection of educational programs and workshops, such as guided tours, lectures, and other types of workshops. These workshops offer participants the chance to engage with museum collections on a deeper level and conduct in-depth explorations of them.

4.4. Electronic Sources of Information

Visitors are able to access instructional materials and resources both when they are physically present at the museum as well as remotely thanks to digital resources such as museum websites, apps, and online databases. These resources offer further data, pictures, and multimedia content to supplement your research.

4.5. Outreach Efforts and Participation in the Community
Several types of community engagement are utilized by numerous museums, including outreach initiatives, partnerships with local educational institutions, and community events. Because of these activities, cultural and educational resources will be made more available and inclusive to a wider audience.

4.6. Diverse Audiences Catered to Through Specialized Education
The educational programming at museums is becoming increasingly adaptable to accommodate a wide variety of audience types. This involves making exhibits more accessible, offering services to visitors who have impairments, and catering to the specific requirements and interests of children, adults, seniors, and other cultural or demographic groups.

5. The Role of Museums in the School System and the Community

5.1. Education in a School Setting
The formal education system is enhanced by museums since they offer a wealth of materials to both professors and students. They act as extensions of the classroom, providing chances for students to participate in research projects, field trips, and other activities that are connected with the curriculum and enhance the overall learning experience.

5.2. Education in an Informal Setting
Informal education is significantly aided by the contributions made by museums. They provide possibilities for learning outside of the traditional classroom context, where individuals can explore and extend their knowledge depending on their interests, and they offer these opportunities to individuals.

Museums are designed to appeal to those who are interested in learning throughout their entire lives, as well as to families, tourists, and curious minds looking for intellectual stimulation.

6. The Role of Museums in the Education System of the Future

6.1. Participation in Digital Activities
The advent of the digital age has resulted in a greater focus being placed on having access to the internet and participating in activities online. Virtual tours, interactive websites, and instructional content that is easily accessible to audiences all over the world are some of the ways that museums are growing their online presence. This digital outreach makes education and accessibility easier to achieve.

6.2. Learning That Never Stops
Adult audiences and senior citizens are becoming increasingly important to museums as they strive to become more educational institutions that promote lifelong

learning. They provide individuals with the tools necessary to continue their intellectual and cultural development throughout their lives by providing educational programming, lectures, and seminars.

6.3. Participation in the Community

By cultivating meaningful relationships with the people who live nearby and responding to the requirements of their communities, museums are trying to become indispensable components of the neighborhoods in which they are located. This strategy helps to cultivate a sense of ownership and welcomeness inside the museum's physical location.

6.4. Intercultural Communication

Museums have the ability to promote cross-cultural communication and interaction. Museums contribute to a deeper understanding of the cultural richness of the world and the significance of cultural diplomacy by displaying the art, history, and culture of many nations.

6.5. Working Together with Various Educational Organizations

In order to develop individualized educational programs and resources, museums are increasingly teaming up with traditional educational institutions like schools and colleges. These relationships make it possible for students and teachers to participate in one-of-a-kind educational experiences.

Museums, which were formerly thought of as places to store riches, have developed into influential educational institutions in recent decades.

They create a connection between the past, the present, and the future by maintaining cultural heritage, engaging various audiences, and influencing the direction education will take in the future. Museums play a crucial role in the process of making learning an experience that is dynamic, immersive, and accessible. This can be accomplished through the use of interpretive exhibits, hands-on activities, digital resources, or community engagement. As we look to the future, museums will continue to transform and become more innovative. This will allow them to have a greater educational impact and serve as key foundations of ongoing education and cultural enrichment in society.

4.1 The educational mission of museums

The purpose of modern museumss, which have developed into active educational institutions, is to include, motivate, and educate visitors of all ages and walks of life. In addition to its historical function as places to store works of art, historical artifacts, and cultural artifacts, museums now play an active role in both official and informal teaching. This in-depth investigation dives into the educational goal of museums, shedding light on their historical development, many types, various educational methodologies, impact on formal and informal education, and their potential to change the future of education.

1. **The opening statement**
   However, the transition of museums into educational institutions is a phenomena that occurred only in more recent times. Museums have a long and illustrious history that dates back to ancient civilizations. The ability of museums to conserve and present items, objects, and works of art is at the heart of their educational purpose. By doing so, museums are able to make history, art, science, and culture accessible to the general public. The function of museums has grown significantly over the years, and many now devote resources to enlightening and entertaining visitors in order to improve the educational experience.
   In this in-depth analysis, we examine the educational mission of museums by looking at the historical development of museums as educational institutions, the various types of museums, the educational strategies that museums use, the impact that museums have on formal and informal education, and the potential that museums have to shape the future of education.
2. **The Evolution of Museums Into Leading Educational Institutions Throughout History**
   2.1 The Age of Enlightenment and the Beginning of the Public Museum Movement
   The Age of Enlightenment, which occurred in Europe during the 17th and 18th centuries, was a critical period in the evolution of museums into educational institutions. Reason, knowledge, and the importance of education were highly valued by philosophers of the Enlightenment period. Because of this, public museums came into being, providing a wider audience with access to art, culture, and other forms of information.
   Prime instances of this change include the British Museum, which was established in 1753, and the Louvre, which first opened its doors to the general public in 1793, during the French Revolution. A break from the private collections owned by monarchs, nobles, and religious organizations, these institutions signaled the beginning of a new era.
   2.2. The Evolution of Educational Practices During the 19th Century
   The 19th century witnessed the beginning of the establishment of museums dedicated to many fields of study, including art, science, history, and others. During this time period, educational reforms were introduced that pushed for the use of museum materials into more traditional types of instruction. Not only were museums transformed into destinations for leisure, but they also evolved into significant resources for academic institutions and teachers.
3. **A Wide Variety of Museums Serving Various Educational Purposes**
   3.1. Art Galleries and Museums
   The Museum of Modern Art (MoMA) in New York and the National Gallery in London are two examples of art museums that provide a comprehensive educational experience that is centered on visual arts. They give spectators the

opportunity to connect with a wide variety of artistic traditions, styles, and techniques. Art museums frequently offer educational programs, exhibitions, and resources aimed not only at the general public but also at more specialized groups.

3.2. Natural Science Galleries and Museums

Visitors at natural history museums, such as the American Museum of Natural History in New York City and the National Museum of Natural History in Washington, District of Columbia, are provided with information regarding the natural world. These establishments maintain extensive collections of biological specimens, fossils, minerals, and anthropological items in their archives and storage facilities. They provide instructional programs that center on topics such as evolution, biodiversity, and the history of the earth.

3.3. Museums Devoted to Science and Technology

The Exploratorium in San Francisco and the Science Museum in London are two examples of science and technology museums that provide visitors the opportunity to participate in hands-on educational activities.

They do this by providing visitors with interactive displays that investigate scientific ideas, technological advancements, and the influence science has on people's everyday lives.

3.4. Museums of Past Civilizations and Cultural Heritage

History museums, such as the National Museum of American History in Washington, District of Columbia, and cultural heritage museums, such as the Acropolis Museum in Athens, demonstrate the historical and cultural wealth of societies. The museums display artifacts, records, and exhibitions that convey the stories of human civilization. As a result, visitors are able to get a more in-depth comprehension of both their own history and the variety of civilizations found across the world.

3.5. Museums That Are Both Unique And Specialized

There are museums that are dedicated to particular subjects or areas of interest. For instance, the International Spy Museum in Washington, District of Columbia, digs into the realm of espionage and provides educational insights into the history of intelligence, as well as security and safety. In a similar vein, unusual museums, such as the Museum of Bad Art in Massachusetts, cultivate unorthodox educational experiences that question standard conceptions of art and culture.

3.6. Online Galleries and the Emergence of the Digital Age

The advent of the digital age has heralded the beginning of a new era of virtual museums, which can be visited via the internet. These institutions provide virtual tours, interactive displays, and digital resources, making it possible for audiences all over the world to experience collections without having to leave the comfort of their own homes. The nature of educational institutions is changing in this day and age, and one example of this is the rise of virtual museums.

4. **Educational Methodologies Employed in Museums**

   4.1. Exhibits With Interpretive Text

   Visitors are kept interested by the use of storytelling, interactive displays, and multimedia components in interpretive exhibits. They enhance the visitor's comprehension of the collection by providing context, historical narratives, and information about the items in the collection.

   4.2. Activities That Involve Your Hands

   Experience-based education is emphasized through the use of hands-on activities in numerous museums. Visitors have the opportunity to touch, experiment, and create, all of which contribute to an enhanced understanding of complicated subjects.

   4.3. Educational Programs and Workshops

   Museums typically provide visitors with a diverse selection of educational programs and workshops, such as docent-led tours, lectures, and interactive workshops. These workshops offer participants the chance to engage with museum collections on a deeper level and conduct in-depth explorations of them.

   4.4. Electronic Sources of Information

   Visitors are able to access instructional materials and resources both when they are physically present at the museum as well as remotely thanks to digital resources such as museum websites, apps, and online databases. These resources offer supplemental information, photos, and multimedia content, which contributes to an overall improvement in the quality of the educational experience.

   4.5. Outreach Efforts and Participation in the Community

   Several types of community engagement are utilized by numerous museums, including outreach initiatives, partnerships with local educational institutions, and community events. As a result of these activities, cultural and educational resources are made more accessible and inclusive; this fosters a sense of ownership and engagement in the museum environment.

   4.6. Diverse Audiences Catered to Through Specialized Education

   The educational programming at museums is becoming increasingly adaptable to accommodate a wide variety of audience types. This involves making exhibits more accessible, offering services to visitors who have impairments, and catering to the specific requirements and interests of children, adults, seniors, and other cultural or demographic groups.

5. **The Role of Museums in the School System and the Community**

   5.1. Education in a School Setting

   The formal education system is enhanced by museums since they offer a wealth of materials to both professors and students. They act as extensions of the classroom, providing chances for students to participate in research projects, field trips, and other activities that are connected with the curriculum and enhance the overall learning experience.

5.2. Education in an Informal Setting

Informal education is significantly aided by the contributions made by museums. They provide possibilities for learning outside of the traditional classroom context, where individuals can explore and extend their knowledge depending on their interests, and they offer these opportunities to individuals.

Museums are designed to appeal to those who are interested in learning throughout their entire lives, as well as to families, tourists, and curious minds looking for intellectual stimulation.

6. The Role of Museums in the Education System of the Future

6.1. Participation in Digital Activities

The advent of the digital age has resulted in a greater focus being placed on having access to the internet and participating in activities online. Virtual tours, interactive websites, and instructional content that is easily accessible to audiences all over the world are some of the ways that museums are growing their online presence. This digital outreach makes education and accessibility easier to achieve.

6.2. Learning That Never Stops

Adult audiences and senior citizens are becoming increasingly important to museums as they strive to become more educational institutions that promote lifelong learning. They provide individuals with the tools necessary to continue their intellectual and cultural development throughout their lives by providing educational programming, lectures, and seminars.

6.3. Participation in the Community

By cultivating meaningful relationships with the people who live nearby and responding to the

requirements of their communities, museums are trying to become indispensable components of the neighborhoods in which they are located. This strategy helps to cultivate a sense of ownership and welcomeness inside the museum's physical location.

6.4. Intercultural Communication

Museums have the ability to promote cross-cultural communication and interaction. Museums contribute to a deeper understanding of the cultural richness of the world and the significance of cultural diplomacy by displaying the art, history, and culture of many nations.

6.5. Working Together with Various Educational Organizations

In order to develop individualized educational programs and resources, museums are increasingly teaming up with traditional educational institutions like schools and colleges. These relationships make it possible for students and teachers to participate in one-of-a-kind learning and research opportunities.

MUSEUMS AND GALLERIES

The traditional function of museums as places to store works of art, historical artifacts, and cultural artifacts has evolved into that of influential educational institutions. They create a connection between the past, the present, and the future by maintaining cultural heritage, engaging various audiences, and influencing the direction education will take in the future. Museums play a crucial role in the process of making learning an experience that is dynamic, immersive, and accessible. This can be accomplished through the use of interpretive exhibits, hands-on activities, digital resources, or community engagement. As we look to the future, museums will continue to transform and become more innovative. This will allow them to have a greater educational impact and serve as key foundations of ongoing education and cultural enrichment in society.

4.2 Educational programs and initiatives

Visitors of all ages and from all walks of life may expect to have their perspectives broadened, their knowledge expanded, and their lives broadened further thanks to the educational programs and initiatives that museums and other cultural institutions have made essential components of their operations. These programs include a diverse array of activities, such as guided tours and seminars, as well as online materials and outreach projects. The overarching goal of these endeavors is to make learning an experience that is both engaging and approachable. at this investigation, we investigate the significance of educational programs at museums, the several categories of programs that can be participated in, the influence that these programs have on both formal and informal education, and the opportunities for new developments in the field.

1. **The opening statement**

   The function of museums as dynamic educational institutions that embrace the job of expanding the visitors' knowledge and supporting lifelong learning has emerged as a result of this evolution. Educational programs and activities are at the core of this transition, providing visitors with opportunity to connect with collections, artifacts, and exhibitions in meaningful and interactive ways. These programs and initiatives are at the heart of this transformation. These programs intend to close the gap between formal and informal education by giving participants from a wide range of backgrounds the opportunity to investigate and deepen their comprehension of topics such as art, history, science, and culture.

   In the course of this in-depth investigation, we will investigate the relevance of educational programs and initiatives in museums, as well as the several types of programs that are now accessible, the impact that these programs have on formal and informal education, and the possibilities for future breakthroughs in this sector.

2. **A Discussion on the Importance of Educational Programs in Museums**

   2.1. Improving the Participation of Visitors

   The goal of museum engagement is to provide guests with experiences that are

both meaningful and memorable. Visitors are given opportunity to engage with the collections in a way that is both interactive and hands-on as part of educational programs, which results in a greater appreciation for and comprehension of the subject matter.

2.2. Providing Opportunities for More In-Depth Exploration

The collections and narratives in museums are typically quite extensive and intricate. Through various educational events, guests are given the opportunity to investigate topics in further detail. The added context, interpretation, and resources that programs provide contribute to an increased level of involvement and comprehension.

2.3. Promoting Education that Lasts a Lifetime

The mission of museums is to be centers of lifelong learning, providing programming for visitors of all ages. The goal of these educational programs is to foster intellectual development and curiosity throughout a person's life by catering to the varying requirements and interests of children, adults, seniors, and lifelong learners.

2.4. Deepening Our Roots Within the Community

More and more, museums are making efforts to become deeply ingrained in the communities that they serve. Educational activities, which may include outreach initiatives, help to establish a sense of ownership in the community, build connections with local citizens, and satisfy the requirements of the group.

2.5. Increasing the Value of Both Formal and Informal Education

Both formal and informal forms of education can be improved with the help of educational programs. They give supplemental learning opportunities outside of the classroom as well as resources and experiences that are aligned with the curricula that are being taught.

3. The Many Forms That Educational Programs and Initiatives Can Take

3.1. Tours Led By Experts

The majority of museums offer some sort of educational program in the form of guided tours.

These tours are typically led by educated educators or docents who provide context, explanation, and insights into the exhibit being viewed. These tours deepen the visitor's appreciation for the objects and exhibitions by increasing their level of comprehension of them.

3.2. Interactive Workshops and Other Participatory Events

Visitors are encouraged to actively engage with the subject matter through the participation in workshops and other hands-on activities. They encourage hands-on learning by having participants engage in activities such as making art, conducting scientific experiments, or taking part in historical reenactments.

3.3. Lectures and Presentations for the Purpose of Education

Opportunities for more in-depth research of issues that are relevant to the museum's holdings are provided in the form of lectures and presentations given by specialists, scholars, and artists. The attendees receive crucial new insights and views as a result of these programs.

3.4. Programs in the Schools

The creation of school programs that are in line with curriculums is a joint effort between educational institutions and museums. These programs frequently consist of guided tours, workshops, and other interactive experiences that are geared toward particular grade levels and topics of study.

3.5. Programs for Families and Young Children

The purpose of family and children's programs is to make museums more approachable and interesting for young visitors and the families that accompany them. Activities geared at children of the right age, as well as interactive exhibitions, are frequently included.

3.6. Digital Resources and Learning Through Online Platforms

The advent of the digital age has resulted in a shift in focus toward online resources as well as distance education. Both visitors who are physically there and those who are not can access supplementary information, photographs, and forms of multimedia content via the websites, applications, and databases that museums make available.

3.7. Engagement with the Community and Partnerships

Outreach programs, partnerships with local schools, and other community events are some of the ways in which museums participate actively with the areas in which they are located. Because of these activities, cultural and educational resources will be made more available and inclusive to a wider audience.

4. The Repercussions for Both Formal and Informal Education

4.1. Education at an Institution

The educational activities that museums offer are designed to supplement the formal education system by providing helpful resources for both students and teachers. They act as extensions of the classroom by providing chances for field trips, research projects, and other programs that are connected with the curriculum and expand the student's experience of learning.

4.2. Education in an Informal Setting

Informal education is significantly aided by the contributions made by museums. They provide possibilities for learning outside of the traditional classroom context, where individuals can explore and extend their knowledge depending on their interests, and they offer these opportunities to individuals. Museums are designed to appeal to those who are interested in learning throughout their entire lives, as well as to families, tourists, and curious minds looking for intellectual stimulation.

4.3. Filling in the Blanks in Terms of Learning

Educational programs in museums fill in the gaps in learning by offering resources and experiences that are aligned with educational curricula and offer supplemental learning opportunities outside of the classroom. Educational programs in museums bridge gaps in learning by providing resources and experiences that match with educational curricula. They encourage a more well-rounded education by appealing to a variety of learning styles and senses.

4.4. Promote Analytical and Creative Thinking by Offering Encouragement

Many educational programs encourage students to engage in creative and critical thinking as well as problem solving. They encourage visitors to question, examine, and apply what they have learned, which results in a more profound and profound comprehension of the subject matter.

5. Upcoming Changes and Improvements to Educational Programs

5.1. Engagement in Digital Forms

A new era of online access and virtual involvement has begun as a direct result of the advent of the digital age. Virtual tours, interactive websites, and instructional content that is easily accessible to audiences all over the world are some of the ways that museums are growing their online presence. This digital outreach makes education and accessibility easier to achieve.

5.2. Learning That Never Stops

Adult audiences and senior citizens are becoming increasingly important to museums as they strive to become more educational institutions that promote lifelong learning. They provide individuals with the tools necessary to continue their intellectual and cultural development throughout their lives by providing educational programming, lectures, and seminars.

5.3. Participation in the Community

By cultivating meaningful relationships with the people who live nearby and responding to the requirements of their communities, museums are trying to become indispensable components of the neighborhoods in which they are located. This strategy helps to cultivate a sense of ownership and welcomeness inside the museum's physical location.

5.4. Intercultural Communication

Museums have the ability to promote cross-cultural communication and interaction. Museums contribute to a deeper understanding of the cultural richness of the world and the significance of cultural diplomacy by displaying the art, history, and culture of many nations.

5.5. Working Together with Various Educational Organizations

In order to develop individualized educational programs and resources, museums are increasingly teaming up with traditional educational institutions like schools and colleges. These relationships make it possible for students and teachers to participate in one-of-a-kind learning and research opportunities.

MUSEUMS AND GALLERIES

It is essential for museums to implement educational programs and activities in order to play a crucial role in elevating visitor engagement, supporting lifelong learning, and increasing depth of understanding. They are extremely important in bridging the gap between formal and informal education as well as in enhancing the overall learning experience. These programs offer a variety of engaging and participatory ways to learn new things, such as through guided tours, workshops, online resources, or community outreach. Learning will become more engaging, accessible, and inclusive for people of all ages and backgrounds if museums continue to innovate and adapt in the years to come. This will ensure that museums play an important part in defining the educational landscape of the future.

4.3 Museums and formal education

Museums now play an increasingly important role in the more traditional forms of education because they offer students, professors, and educational institutions access to a wealth of useful information. These cultural institutions provide a learning environment that is both distinctive and immersive, and they do so as a supplement to the more conventional classroom setting. In the course of this investigation, we will investigate the significance of museums in traditional education, the numerous ways in which they complement curriculum, the influence on student learning, and the possibilities for further integrating museums into the traditional education system.

1. **The opening statement**

   Formal education, which often takes place within the more regimented environments of schools and classrooms, is what enables individuals to acquire the foundational information and skills necessary for both academic and personal development. However, expanding the learning experience beyond the constraints of the classroom can considerably enhance its quality and make it more meaningful. The emergence of museums as significant partners in formal education can be attributed to the museums' ability to provide students with opportunities to engage with subjects such as history, science, art, and culture that are both dynamic and engaging. These cultural institutions offer students access to materials and experiences that bolster educational programs, foster critical thinking, and incite a passion of learning that lasts a lifetime.

   In this in-depth investigation, we will investigate the role that museums play in formal education, the numerous ways in which museums assist educational curriculum, the influence that museums have on the educational experiences of students, and the opportunities that exist for further integrating museums into the formal education system.

2. **The Importance of Museums in the Conventional Educational System**

   2.1. Applications in the Real World

   Students get the opportunity to apply what they have learned in the classroom to situations that occur in the real world when they visit museums. Students are able to better understand how academic information is applied in real life when they have the opportunity to engage with artifacts, exhibitions, and experts from a variety of fields.

2.2. Learning Through Multiple Senses

Museums appeal to a variety of senses, providing visitors with an educational experience that is multimodal. Students are able to perceive the subject matter through their senses of touch, sight, hearing, and occasionally even smell and taste. This strategy incorporates many senses, which helps improve memory retention as well as comprehension.

2.3. The Enhancement of Instructional Programs

The collections and exhibits shown in museums frequently correspond to the objectives of various educational courses. They provide additional context, historical narratives, and facts that augment classroom learning, thereby improving students' grasp of the subject matter that is being studied.

2.4. Thinking Critically and Engaging in Inquiry

Students are encouraged to think critically and ask questions when visiting museums. Students are forced to analyze, evaluate, and apply the knowledge they have gained, which helps them develop critical thinking abilities, which are essential for both academic and personal development.

2.5. Learning That Never Stops

Museums strive to instill in visitors a passion of learning that will last a lifetime. By encouraging students to participate in a dynamic and interactive manner, museums spread the message that learning is not limited to what is taught in a classroom setting and should be viewed as a lifelong pursuit.

3. The Many Ways Museums Contribute to Conventional Education

3.1. Programs That Are Aligned With The Curriculum

A great number of museums provide educational programs that have been thoughtfully

developed to complement the curriculums of local schools. These programs may consist of workshops, guided tours, and other interactive experiences that are geared specifically toward the grade levels and topics of the participants.

3.2. Excursions in the Field

Visits to local museums are a regular component of more conventional forms of schooling. Students are given the opportunity to go to a museum and interact with collections and displays that are related to the subject matter that they are studying. During field visits, students frequently participate in both guided tours and hands-on activities.

3.3. Materials for the Instructors

Museums make available to teachers a wealth of useful resources that can be used to supplement their teaching efforts. This may involve the provision of lesson plans, educational materials, and access to specialists who are able to offer advice and direction.

3.4. Collaboration with Educational Institutions

There has been a recent uptick in cooperative efforts between museums and schools to develop individualized educational programming and materials. Because of these connections, educators are given the opportunity to include museum visits into their lesson plans.

3.5. Interdisciplinary Education and Learning

Students are generally encouraged to make connections between different subjects when they attend museum programs since museums frequently foster interdisciplinary learning. For the purpose of promoting an all-encompassing comprehension of the topic, a museum dedicated to scientific research can, for instance, investigate the background and practice of scientific investigation.

4. The Influence on the Education of the Students

4.1. Increased Capacity for Retention

Memory is improved by the use of several senses throughout the learning process that occurs in museums. Students have a much better chance of remembering the information they acquire through active investigation and engagement with others.

4.2. Enhanced Comprehending

Museums provide students with additional context and interpretation, both of which increase their grasp of the material being studied. They demonstrate how academic principles can be used in the actual world, which makes the subject matter more applicable and tangible.

4.3. Capacity for Analytical and Critical Thinking

Students are encouraged to engage in critical thinking and inquiry when they visit museums. They help students develop their analytical skills and encourage them to assess and put their information to use, both of which are important for academic achievement.

4.4. A Source of Motivation for Ongoing Education

Students frequently find the motivation to continue their education through engagement with museums. A trip to a museum can serve as the impetus for further investigation into the topic at hand in the form of independent study and investigation.

5. The Ongoing Participation of Museums in Traditional Educational Settings

5.1. Electronic Sources of Information

The advent of the digital age has presented museums with fresh options to broaden their audience base. Virtual tours and online tools that can be included into the conventional educational system are becoming an increasingly common feature at museums.

5.2. Learning That Never Stops

Students are being encouraged to develop a passion for continuous education through the efforts of museums. This may result in a change in strategy taken by the educational system in order to promote learning that is both self-directed and ongoing.

5.3. Partnerships with the Community

The formal education experience is being actively sought to be improved by museums as they actively attempt to become essential parts of their communities. This may include more engagement with local schools and educational institutions to improve the quality of formal education.

5.4. Intercultural Communication and Inclusiveness

By presenting the artwork, historical artifacts, and cultural practices of a wide variety of societies, museums have the potential to promote cultural understanding and acceptance. This contributes to a deeper comprehension of the cultural diversity that exists around the world as well as the significance of cultural diplomacy.

The role of museums in formal education has grown significantly in recent years, as they now provide students with access to a wealth of useful resources and educational opportunities. They provide an atmosphere for learning that engages multiple senses, which improves one's ability to remember information, comprehend it, and think critically. Students are encouraged to view education as an ongoing adventure and to develop a passion of learning that will last a lifetime when they visit museums. Students will have access to richer, more dynamic, and more engaging learning experiences that go beyond the four walls of the classroom if museums continue to innovate and broaden the scope of their services. There is a great possibility for museums to become more fully integrated into the official education system.

4.4 The role of museums in promoting lifelong learning

By providing dynamic and immersive experiences that encourage curiosity, critical thinking, and a constant desire for knowledge throughout an individual's life, museums play an important role in the promotion of lifelong learning. This is because museums play a significant role in encouraging lifelong learning. These cultural institutions, with their varied collections and engaging programming, cultivate a profound and enduring love of learning that stretches far beyond what is taught in a typical classroom setting. In this article, we investigate the myriad ways in which museums contribute to the promotion of lifelong learning.

1. **Interested Curiosity and Active Participation**

   The purpose of museums is to stimulate visitors' natural sense of wonder and to keep their
   attention throughout their visit. Museums offer an atmosphere in which people of all ages are encouraged to investigate, question, and look for answers. This can be accomplished through the medium of detailed artworks, historical artifacts, or interactive exhibitions. People who have a natural interest for a wide variety

of topics are more likely to pursue lifelong learning because it motivates them to investigate those topics further.

2. **Learning Through Multiple Senses**
   The stimulation of a number of senses contributes to the overall depth of the educational experience provided by museums. The learning experience is made more memorable and exciting for the visitors by providing opportunities for them to see, touch, hear, and sometimes even smell and taste the subject matter. This multisensory method caters to a variety of learning styles and facilitates a more in-depth comprehension of the subject matter.

3. **The promotion of analytical and deductive reasoning**
   Visitors are encouraged to think critically and analytically when they are in museums. They inspire individuals to critically assess information, create connections, and draw their own conclusions. This emphasis on critical thinking not only leads to a more profound comprehension, but it also provides individuals with a valuable talent that can be used for further education.

4. **A Wide Range of Educational Opportunities**
   The educational programs and resources provided by museums are diverse and can be adapted to meet the needs of visitors of varying ages and levels of interest. Museums offer a plethora of learning possibilities that are designed to accommodate to a variety of learning preferences. These opportunities include lecture series, hands-on workshops, guided tours, and digital resources.

5. **Availability of Knowledge and Skills**
   Educators and subject matter experts who are able to share their ideas and knowledge on a wide variety of topics are frequently found working in museums. This access to expertise enriches the learning process and encourages individuals, throughout their life, to seek out experts and mentors in the fields in which they are interested.

6. **Initiatives for Continuous Lifelong Learning**
   The idea of learning throughout one's life is supported and actively promoted by a great number of museums, which demonstrate this support through the provision of a variety of programs and activities aimed specifically at adults and seniors. These programs urge individuals to continue their intellectual and cultural progress long into their elder years, especially if they are already well into their later years.

7. **Participation in the Community**
   The goal of museums is to become indispensable components of the communities that they serve. They maintain strong relationships with the local populace, as well as schools and community organizations. This interaction helps to cultivate a sense of ownership and inclusivity in the museum environment, so making learning more accessible to everyone.

8. **Intercultural Communication and Affirmation of Difference**

Museums frequently exhibit the artwork, historical artifacts, and cultural practices of a wide range of societies, which helps to promote intercultural dialogue and acceptance. This promotes a broader awareness of global diversity by encouraging life-long learners to investigate and appreciate the cultural richness of the world's many different nations and peoples.

Chapter 5

Museums and Cultural Heritage

Explore the profound connection between museums and cultural heritage, the role of museums in protecting and presenting cultural heritage, as well as the obstacles and opportunities in this significant sector. By all means, let's delve into the complex and rich relationship that exists between cultural heritage and museums.

1. **The opening statement**
   The purpose of museums is to function as stewards of cultural heritage by collecting, preserving, and exhibiting artifacts, works of art, and historical items that are representative of a variety of different societies and civilizations. This in-depth investigation will delve into the multifaceted relationship between museums and cultural heritage, highlighting the significance of cultural heritage preservation, the role of museums in safeguarding and interpreting cultural artifacts, the challenges faced in preserving cultural heritage, and the evolving approaches to promote cultural heritage awareness and inclusivity. Specifically, this investigation will focus on the role of museums in safeguarding and interpreting cultural artifacts.
2. **The Importance of Preserving Cultural Heritage**
   The physical and intangible parts of a society's history, traditions, and values are the components that make up its cultural heritage. This heritage is representative of the community's collective identity and its legacy. A rich tapestry of human civilization is reflected in its archeological sites, historical monuments, artifacts, artworks, cultural activities, rituals, languages, and oral traditions, all of which are included in this concept. The preservation of cultural heritage acts as a repository for information, illuminating the process of social evolution while also promoting a more profound comprehension of the common experiences we all have as humans.

3. **The Importance of Museums to the Maintenance of Cultural Heritage**
   3.1. Collection and Preservation of Artifacts
   Museums are responsible for the acquisition, cataloging, and curation of cultural relics and artworks. This ensures the objects' continued existence for future generations. They apply specialized techniques for conservation in order to safeguard fragile objects and ensure that their integrity is preserved over time.
   3.2. Research and Explanatory Analysis
   In order to understand and place cultural items in their appropriate context, museums engage in considerable research and intellectual investigations. They work along with historians, archaeologists, and other specialists to give in-depth narratives that illuminate the social, cultural, and historical relevance of the objects in their collections.
   3.3. Exhibits and Displays Open to the Public
   Museums frequently host exhibitions and shows in order to present historical relics and artistic creations to the general audience. These exhibitions serve as educational platforms that encourage dialogue and involvement, so contributing to the development of a greater awareness of cultural heritage among a variety of audiences.
   3.4. Programs of Education and Community Outreach
   The purpose of educational programs and community outreach efforts developed by museums is to raise awareness of cultural heritage and to foster an inclusive environment. These programs encourage involvement, cultivate a sense of ownership, and instill a sense of pride in cultural heritage. They are aimed at schools, communities, and a variety of demographic groups.
4. **Obstacles Facing the Conservation of Cultural Heritage**
   4.1. Preserving and Restoring the Environment
   The problem that museums face is preserving and repairing historical locations and objects that are in a state of deterioration. To ensure the cultural legacy is preserved for future generations, this calls for the application of sustainable conservation strategies, as well as specialist knowledge and resources.
   4.2. Finances and Available Resources
   When it comes to the upkeep and preservation of cultural relics, museums frequently face challenges related to insufficient money and resources. It is absolutely necessary, in order to continue the protection of cultural assets, to both successfully get long-term funding and to put efficient resource management plans into action.
   4.3. The Effects of Climate Change and Other Environmental Factors
   The adverse effects of climate change on cultural heritage sites and artifacts can be seen in the form of deterioration of the surrounding environment, erosion, and the disappearance of important historical markers.
   It is imperative that museums respond to the effects of climate change by taking

preventative conservation measures and engaging in environmentally responsible operations.

4.4. The Protection of the Cultural Heritage

The protection of cultural assets against unlawful activities such as looting, excavation, and trading is a problem to museums. In order to accomplish this goal, there must be collaboration on a global scale, support for legislation that safeguard cultural heritage, and the implementation of rigorous regulations to combat the illegal trafficking of cultural items.

5. **Evolving Methodologies for the Preservation of Cultural Heritage**

5.1. Technology and the Preservation of Digital Content

To build digital copies of cultural items and heritage locations, museums are utilizing technology for digital preservation projects, such as scanning in three dimensions (3D), virtual reality, and digital archiving. These technical breakthroughs assure that future generations will have access to cultural heritage and that it will be preserved.

5.2. Engagement with the Community and Collaborative Efforts

By inviting local people to participate in programs to preserve cultural heritage, museums are helping to cultivate community participation and collaboration. This collaborative approach encourages a sense of ownership and responsibility among people of the community, which in turn fosters practices that are sustainable for the preservation of cultural property.

5.3. The Promotion of the Safeguarding of Cultural Heritage

Museums are leading the charge to have international regulations and agreements enacted that will protect cultural heritage and crack down on illegal trafficking of such items. They work together with governmental and non-governmental organizations to educate people about the need of preserving cultural objects and historical sites, as well as to enforce rules that do so.

5.4. Including Everyone and Being Represented

In the process of preserving and interpreting cultural history, museums are making efforts to encourage diversity and representation in their visitor experiences. They are engaging a variety of communities and groups who have been historically marginalized in order to guarantee that their narratives and voices will be represented and protected within the cultural heritage discourse.

6. **Social Identity and the Importance of Cultural Heritage**

The values, practices, and ideas that are held in common by a community are reflected in its cultural legacy, which is inextricably connected to social identity. Museums are aware of the significance of cultural heritage in maintaining the intangible parts of human civilization, establishing a sense of connection and pride among communities, and promoting cultural diversity.

7. **The Impact of Globalization on Cultural Patrimony**

In a world that is becoming more globalized, it is more important than ever to preserve our cultural legacy in order to protect the diverse nations' ability to maintain their individual identities and customs. The promotion of cultural interchange, the promotion of intercultural discussion, and the preservation of cultural legacy are all extremely important roles that museums perform, and they play these roles extremely well.

Museums have an important role as stewards of cultural heritage, preserving and interpreting the diverse fabric of human history for the benefit of both the current generation and future generations. They play an essential part in increasing awareness, promoting inclusivity, and fostering a greater knowledge of the relevance of cultural heritage in shaping social identity and promoting cultural diversity, all of which contribute to the larger goal of fostering cultural variety. Museums continue to employ creative strategies and collaborative initiatives to ensure the sustainable conservation and protection of cultural items and historical locations, despite the problems that are faced in the process of safeguarding cultural heritage. Museums provide a significant contribution to the ongoing global endeavor to preserve the many legacy of human civilization for future generations by encouraging a widespread understanding of the world's diverse cultural traditions.

5.1 The preservation of cultural heritage in museums

It is the responsibility of museums to protect and conserve this cultural heritage for the benefit of future generations. Cultural heritage can be defined as a society's shared identity, history, and artistic expressions. The role of museums as stewards of our collective cultural heritage includes the conservation of artifacts, historical objects, works of art, and other tangible and intangible facets of culture. This all-encompassing investigation digs into the important features of cultural heritage preservation within museums, including the relevance of preservation, techniques and procedures, obstacles faced, and the growing approaches that ensure the conservation and protection of our cultural inheritance.

1. **The opening statement**

   The tangible and intangible elements of a society's history, traditions, and ideals are all included in its cultural heritage to varying degrees. A rich tapestry of human civilization is reflected in its archeological sites, historical monuments, artifacts, artworks, cultural activities, rituals, languages, and oral traditions, all of which are included in this concept.

   The protection of our historical and cultural heritage is absolutely necessary if we are to ensure the continuity of our common past and identity.

   Because they are the keepers of both cultural artifacts and information, museums are an essential component in the process of cultural heritage preservation. They seek out, collect, preserve, and give explanations for historical artifacts and practices, all with the goal of handing them on to subsequent generations. This extensive investigation will provide an in-depth analysis of the preservation of cultural heritage within museums, focusing on its significance, the techniques and methods employed, the challenges faced, and the evolving approaches to ensure the conservation and protection of our cultural legacy. This will be accomplished by examining the evolution of these methods to ensure the preservation of our cultural legacy.

2. **The Importance of Attempting to Preserve Our Cultural Heritage**
   2.1. Keeping One's Cultural Identity Alive and Well
   The cultural history of a community, region, or nation is inextricably linked to that group's or nation's sense of self. It is a representation of the shared history, values, and customs that have played a role in the formation of the distinct identity of a given group. Preserving something ensures that it will continue to exist in its original form for future as well as current generations.

   2.2. Cultivating a Feeling of Belonging in Others
   The preservation of a community's cultural history fosters a sense of pride and belonging among its members. Individuals are able to establish a connection with their ancestry and roots when they have access to this resource, which acts as a source of cultural and national identity. Keeping important cultural items and rituals alive helps members of a community feel more connected to one another.

   2.3. Education and enlightenment
   The study of one's cultural heritage can be both educational and enlightening. The public's education about their history, traditions, and values is significantly aided by the presence of museums in their communities. This educational component is essential to the development of a more profound appreciation for the variety of human cultures and the role that heritage plays in shaping the human experience.

   2.4. Scholarship and Academic Research
   The preservation of cultural legacy is beneficial to the fields of history, archaeology, anthropology, and art history, as well as to study and scholarship in those fields. To investigate the past and get new understandings from it, academics and researchers rely on artifacts and records that have been preserved.

   2.5. Supporting a Rich and Diverse Cultural Landscape
   The cultural heritage of a society exemplifies the multifarious and complex nature of human
   communities. The maintenance of this history fosters an understanding of cultural diversity as well as the peaceful coexistence of a variety of customs, languages, and artistic manifestations.

3. **Methods and Techniques of Archival Preservation**
   3.1. Protection and Reconstruction
   The act of preserving cultural heritage includes important components such

as conservation and restoration. Conservators are experts in repairing and preserving fragile things, artworks, and historical locations by employing a variety of specialized techniques. This includes stabilizing artifacts using non-invasive means in addition to cleaning and mending the artifacts.

3.2. Regulation of the Environment

For the purpose of preserving artifacts, it is essential to keep the environment consistent. The preservation of cultural artifacts often requires museums to carefully monitor and regulate environmental factors such as temperature, humidity, and lighting. The preservation of antiquities in pristine form is made possible by these carefully managed environments.

3.3. Documentation and Cataloguing

Documenting and organizing the museum's collection of artifacts requires painstaking attention to detail. Records that are detailed contain information about an object's history, including its status and any past treatments it may have had. For the purpose of tracing an item's history and assuring that the thing will be preserved, this documentation is absolutely necessary.

3.4. Safety and Adequate Protection

Theft and vandalism are two of the primary threats that museums face, so they take precautions to secure their holdings. For the purpose of protecting cultural objects, we use surveillance equipment, security personnel, and access that is strictly regulated.

3.5. Digitization as well as Archiving in the Digital Format

The development of new technologies has made it possible for museums to generate digital copies and archives of the collections they house. This type of digital preservation ensures that cultural artifacts are available to researchers and the general public, therefore reducing the amount of handling and exposure that physical objects are subjected to.

4. Obstacles to Be Confronted When Preserving Cultural Heritage

4.1. Insufficient Available Funding

Many museums struggle with budgetary issues that make it difficult for them to preserve their collections. The preservation of collections, as well as their protection and monitoring, as well as their digitization, all require financial support. It is absolutely necessary to have reliable sources of financial support.

4.2. Impacts on the Environment and the Changing Climate

The effects of climate change can be catastrophic for the sites and objects that make up a country's cultural heritage. The threat to historical landmarks and cultural goods comes from multiple sources, including rising sea levels, extreme weather events, and pollution. It is imperative that museums consider the effects of climate change on the preservation of cultural assets.

4.3. Preservation of the Cultural Heritage

Illegal excavation, theft, and sale in stolen cultural artifacts pose a threat to cultural heritage. Illegal trade in cultural objects poses a risk to the protection of cultural heritage, necessitating collaboration on a global scale and lobbying efforts geared toward the preservation of cultural property.

4.4. Obstacles Presented by Technology

Although new opportunities for digital preservation are presented by technological advancements, there are also new challenges. The lightning-fast pace at which digital formats and platforms are being updated might create access and compatibility problems in the long run.

5. **Evolving Methodologies for the Preservation of Cultural Heritage**

5.1. Technology and the Preservation of Digital Content

Technology is being utilized by museums in order to generate digital representations of historical artifacts and locations. 3D scanning, virtual reality, and digital archiving make it possible for researchers and the general public to access cultural material while simultaneously reducing the amount of physical handling that is required.

5.2. Engagement with the Community and Collaborative Efforts

The participation of local communities in museum preservation activities is being encouraged. This method promotes a sense of ownership and responsibility among community members as well as supports the use of sustainable techniques for the purpose of preserving cultural property.

5.3. The Promotion of the Safeguarding of Cultural Heritage

There is a concerted effort made by museums to lobby for national and international legislation and agreements that safeguard cultural assets. They work together with governmental and non-governmental organizations to educate people about the need of preserving cultural objects and historical sites, as well as to enforce rules that do so.

5.4. Including Everyone and Being Represented

In the process of preserving cultural history, museums are making efforts to encourage diversity and representation of a diverse range of people. They are engaging a variety of communities and groups who have been historically marginalized in order to guarantee that their narratives and voices will be represented and protected within the cultural heritage discourse.

The protection of our collective history, identity, and values is an activity that is of the utmost importance, and museums serve as the keepers of this important information. They play an essential part in the preservation of cultural objects as well as the interpretation of those items, the provision of educational platforms, and the promotion of a sense of belonging and pride among communities. Museums continue to embrace new strategies and collaborative activities to ensure the sustained conservation and protection of our cultural history. This is the case even though there are many obstacles to overcome when it comes to the preservation of cultural property. Museums provide a significant contribution to the ongoing global endeavor to preserve the many legacy of human civilization for future generations by encouraging a widespread understanding of the world's diverse cultural traditions.

5.2 The repatriation debate

The argument over repatriation is a complicated and emotionally fraught issue that centers on the return of cultural items, human remains, and religious objects to the communities to which they belong or to the regions where they were originally discovered. This argument is being fanned by the tension that exists between the rights of indigenous peoples and nations to reclaim their cultural patrimony and the preservation of cultural heritage in museums as a form of cultural preservation. During this in-depth investigation, we will delve into the issue around repatriation and investigate its historical backdrop, the arguments on both sides, the legal and ethical frameworks, as well as the difficulties and repercussions of repatriation.

1. **The opening statement**

   The argument over repatriation lies at the crossroads of several different topics, including the protection of cultural heritage, the rights of indigenous groups, and ethical considerations. It revolves around the topic of whether or not cultural relics, such as paintings, human remains, and religious objects, should be returned to the communities from which they were taken or to the places where they originated.

   This discussion is important from a historical, legal, and ethical standpoint all at the same time. It frequently involves establishments such as museums, universities, and government agencies that house extensive collections of cultural items, such as in the previous sentence. The rights of indigenous peoples are at the center of this controversy. Indigenous peoples believe that the removal of these items, which frequently occurred as a result of colonization and the use of force, constitutes a breach of their cultural identity and history.

2. **The Controversial Issue of Repatriation in its Historical Context**

   The controversy over repatriation has deep historical origins, many of which may be traced back to colonial centuries when indigenous tribes' cultural objects and human remains were stolen without their consent. These migrations were frequently the consequence of military conquest, scientific missions, operations related to missionary work, and commercial endeavors. The items eventually found their way into museums, colleges, and private collections all across the world, where they became an essential part of the study of cultural heritage and its preservation.

   The argument over repatriation gained steam as countries grew more aware of the repercussions of colonialism and the toll it took on indigenous communities. Indigenous groups started to demand the repatriation of their cultural property, human remains, and sacred objects, and they were frequently aided in this endeavor by international organizations and countries that were sympathetic to their cause.

3. **The Cases for and Against Repatriation**
   3.1. Respect for One's Own Culture and Dignity
   Repatriation advocates contend that cultural items should be returned to their original locations since they are an integral component of the cultural identity and dignity of a community. The right of indigenous tribes to control and maintain their cultural heritage should be acknowledged by returning these things.
   3.2. Compensation and Vendor Accountability
   Repatriation is often considered as a means of making amends and getting justice for wrongs committed in the past. It recognizes the historical injustices that were committed against indigenous peoples throughout the time of colonization and it recognizes the right of indigenous people to regain their cultural heritage.
   3.3. Rights of Human Beings
   The discussion on repatriation is situated within the framework of human rights, more specifically the United Nations Declaration on the Rights of Indigenous Peoples (UNDRIP). The United Nations Declaration on the Rights of Indigenous Peoples (UNDRIP) acknowledges the right of indigenous peoples to preserve, control, conserve, and develop their cultural heritage.
   3.4. The Care and Maintenance of Sacred Objects
   In the case of sacred objects, repatriation is frequently regarded as required in order to guarantee that these things be treated with the reverence and respect that they are due within the context of the cultural traditions and rituals that they were originally associated with.
   3.5. The Promotion of Cultural Efforts
   The return of cultural items can help indigenous groups with their cultural revival and preservation efforts, which in turn helps with the transmission of traditional knowledge and practices to subsequent generations.
4. **The Cases Against Being Able to Return Home**
   4.1. Safeguarding the Heritage of the World
   The argument made by museums and other types of institutions is that they serve as worldwide repositories of cultural history. They say that they do this by maintaining and safeguarding objects for the benefit of all of humanity. It's possible that returning artifacts would deprive future generations of the chance to learn about and enjoy our common legacy.
   4.2. Ownership and the Existence of Legal Structures
   It is possible for the ownership of cultural items to create legal complexities; therefore, museums frequently declare that they obtained their collections in a lawful manner. The procedure of demonstrating that one is the rightful owner can be difficult and time consuming.
   4.3. Expertise and Curation of Content

The argument put out by museums is that they are the only institutions that have the necessary knowledge and resources to properly care and preserve cultural items. They feel that they are able to offer an environment that is secure and stable for these things, which may not be achievable in some of the sites where they originated.

4.4. Opportunities and Threats Facing Communities

Repatriation can provide a number of issues for indigenous people, not the least of which is the requirement for adequate storage, preservation, and management of items that have been repatriated. It also has the potential to rise to disagreements within communities over who has the authority to claim cultural property and take care of it.

4.5. The Influence on Academic Study and Research

The return of cultural objects can have repercussions for both educational and scientific endeavors. Some people believe that future generations of researchers and students ought to have access to these artifacts because they are important for comprehending the history, culture, and artistic expressions of other nations and because they should be accessible.

5. The Existence of Both Legal and Ethical Frameworks

5.1. UNDRIP is an abbreviation for the United Nations Declaration on the Rights of Indigenous Peoples

The United Nations Declaration on the Rights of Indigenous Peoples (UNDRIP) acknowledges the rights of indigenous peoples to control, preserve, and advance their cultural heritage. It highlights their right to repatriate property that was taken from them without their consent, including cultural, religious, and spiritual items.

5.2. Global Agreements And Conventions

Guidelines for the restitution of stolen or illegally acquired cultural property can be found in international accords such as the UNESCO Convention on the Means of Prohibiting and Preventing the Illicit Import, Export, and Transfer of Ownership of Cultural Property.

5.3. Legislation at the National Level

Several countries' legislatures have passed laws to address problems associated with repatriation. The Native American Graves Protection and Repatriation Act (NAGPRA), for instance, was enacted in the United States in order to make it easier for indigenous tribes to receive human remains and cultural items that have been returned to them.

6. The Obstacles and Consequences Involved in Repatriation

6.1. Research on the Provenance

A lengthy and difficult procedure, determining the legitimate ownership of cultural artifacts and their provenance can be time-consuming and difficult. It frequently calls for a great deal of research, in addition to collaboration between various institutions and native people.

6.2 Striking a Balance Between Preserving and Protecting Rights

Finding a solution that allows for the protection of cultural heritage while also recognizing and honoring the legal rights of indigenous populations is a difficult task. The potential benefits of repatriation have to be weighed against the museum's responsibility to preserve our collective cultural history.

6.3. The Influence on the Collections

Repatriation has the potential to have a substantial impact on museum collections, which may result in the loss of important objects. It is possible that institutions may need to rethink their policies on the acquisition and deaccessioning of resources.

6.4. What This Means for Potential Future Acquisitions

The argument about repatriation may have consequences for upcoming acquisitions made by museums and other types of institutions. It could result in stricter criteria for acquisitions and improved transparency in collecting operations. Both of these things would be beneficial.

6.5. Consideration of Other Cultures

The discussion over repatriation sheds attention on the importance of demonstrating cultural sensitivity and working together with indigenous people to find solutions to the thorny problems that are associated with the process of repatriation.

The argument over repatriation is a complex and multi-dimensional subject that seeks to strike a balance between the protection of indigenous groups' rights and the preservation of cultural legacy.

It is an important step in acknowledging historical injustices and affirming the rights of indigenous peoples to control, protect, and promote their cultural legacy; nonetheless, it frequently involves difficult legal, ethical, and logistical challenges. A process that is continuing and ever-evolving, finding a balance that respects the rights of indigenous populations while also protecting the world's shared cultural heritage is a vital component of cultural heritage management and ethical responsibility.

5.3 Museums and cultural diplomacy

The use of cultural exchanges, artistic expression, and preservation of cultural traditions as a tool for promoting international understanding, cooperation, and goodwill is the essence of the technique known as "cultural diplomacy." When it comes to the advancement of cultural diplomacy on a worldwide scale, museums, in their capacity as repository of cultural riches and expressions, play a key role. They act as bridges between different cultures, fostering conversation, education, and the sharing of ideas with one another. We will delve into the significant role that museums play in cultural diplomacy, the historical context of cultural exchange, the impact on international relations, as well as the shifting landscape of cultural diplomacy in the digital era as part of this in-depth investigation.

1. **The opening statement**
   The use of cultural diplomacy as a tool to advance intercultural understanding and cooperation between states is a dynamic and effective strategy. Building bridges and fostering stronger ties is accomplished via the sharing of perspectives, customs, artistic expressions, and heritage. Museums, as establishments devoted to the preservation and exhibition of cultural heritage, are appropriate partners in the practice of cultural diplomacy because of their mission statements.
   In the course of this in-depth investigation, we will dig into the myriad of roles that museums play in the process of cultural diplomacy. We will investigate the historical context of cultural exchange, the significance of museums as cultural ambassadors, the impact of cultural diplomacy on foreign relations, as well as the changing environment in the age of digital technology.
2. **The Historic Context of Cross-Cultural Interaction**
   Examples of people from other cultures exchanging ideas and practices can be found all the way back to the earliest known civilizations. These interactions were frequently made possible by commerce, travel, and conquest; they played a key part in the diffusion of art, knowledge, and ideas; and they were often encouraged by these activities.
   2.1. Route de la Soie
   The Silk Road was a network of commercial routes that connected East and West, and it was essential in fostering cultural interaction for hundreds of years. It not only made possible the trading of products, but also of ideas, artistic expressions, and religious convictions. The items and works of art that moved along these routes may be tracked by museums, providing invaluable insight into the cultural exchanges that took place.
   2.2. The Age of the Renaissance
   In Europe during the Renaissance period, there was a resurgence of interest in ancient antiquity. This enthusiasm was in part fostered by the importation of classical artwork and texts from the Byzantine Empire during this time period. This exchange of cultural ideas was an essential factor in the development of the Renaissance movement.
   2.3. Colonialism and the Transmission of Culture
   Colonization frequently involves the gathering of works of art, antiquities, and other cultural
   items from the areas that were conquered. These artifacts were sent to the colonial powers and frequently ended up in museums after being shipped there. Even though this process involved exploitation, it also served as the beginning of a type of cultural exchange.
3. **Museums' Role as Global Cultural Representatives**
   3.1. Protecting and Presenting the Country's Cultural Heritage
   Museums serve to both preserve and display the cultural history of their

respective nations. Their collections showcase the creative, historical, and scientific accomplishments of a wide range of civilizations. As a result, they provide a glimpse into the myriad ways in which humans can express their creativity.

3.2. Promoting Mutual Communication and Comprehending

Museums are places that offer visitors the opportunity to interact with the histories, customs, and traditions of a variety of civilizations. They encourage conversation and comprehension, which contributes to the dismantling of cultural barriers and preconceptions.

3.3. Educational Programs and Exhibitions

Exhibitions, cultural programs, and other events that foster a better knowledge of other cultures are frequently hosted by museums. These initiatives may take the form of art exhibitions, cultural festivals, or lectures that are centered on topics that pertain to the entire world.

3.4. Making It Easier For People To Work Together From Other Countries

It is common practice for museums to work together with their colleagues in other nations. These kinds of partnerships can result in the creation of collaborative exhibitions, academic exchanges, and cultural activities that help to enhance ties between nations.

4. Influence on the Relationships Between Countries

The field of cultural diplomacy, in which museums play a pivotal role, has a significant influence on the state of international relations.

4.1. Establishing Credibility and Goodwill

The exchange of cultural goods is an important component of cultural diplomacy. Understanding and empathy are fostered as a result, both of which are necessary qualities for maintaining peaceful coexistence and diplomatic relations.

4.2. Influence and Other Forms of Soft Power

A nation's attractiveness and culture can be exploited as a sort of soft power through the practice of cultural diplomacy. This allows a nation to change perceptions and affect international relations. When it comes to projecting a nation's soft power through their cultural assets, museums are an extremely important component.

4.3. The Resolution of Conflicts

Through the facilitation of possibilities for communication and mutual comprehension between warring parties, cultural diplomacy can play a role in the process of conflict resolution. Exchanges of cultures are one way to help establish bridges and find common ground.

4.4 Fostering a Sense of National Identity

On the global arena, states are able to more effectively promote their own identities, values, and traditions through the use of cultural diplomacy. It also has the potential to be a platform for challenging preconceived notions and preconceptions.

5. The Shifting Terrain of Cultural Diplomacy in the Age of the Digital Revolution

5.1. Online Museums and Exhibits that Can Be Visited Virtually

Through the use of online exhibitions and virtual tours, museums have been given the ability to communicate with people all over the world. By making art and legacy available to people all around the world, this accessibility contributes to the promotion of cultural diplomacy.

5.2. Participation in Cultural Activities Via Social Media

Through the usage of social media platforms, museums are able to interact with audiences all around the world. They are able to make use of these platforms so that others may view their collections, they can promote cultural exchange, and they can facilitate conversation.

5.3. Online Representations of Cultural Activities

The advent of the digital era has led to the proliferation of cultural gatherings that take place online, such as online music festivals, art exhibitions, and movie screenings. These gatherings make it possible for people from different cultures to interact without any physical barriers.

5.4. Digital Projects Carried Out in Collaboration

Museums and other cultural institutions often work together on digital projects that further the goals of cultural diplomacy. These projects might take a variety of forms, such as digital forums for intercultural discourse or online catalogs of cultural artifacts.

6. Obstacles and Factors to Consider When Engaging in Cultural Diplomacy

6.1. Limitations Imposed by Political and Economic Factors

The practice of cultural diplomacy can be influenced in various ways by political and economic concerns. The available resources for cultural exchange may be restricted due to economic constraints, while the ability to collaborate may be hampered by political issues.

6.2. Sensitivity to Other Cultures

To engage effectively in cultural diplomacy, one must possess both cultural sensitivity and a grasp of the myriad of distinct values, beliefs, and traditions held by various cultures. In this context, careless mistakes might easily lead to misunderstandings or even offense.

6.3 Striking a Balance Between Representations

For the sake of cultural diplomacy, museums ought to strike a balance in their representations. They have a responsibility to make sure that the viewpoints and views of the communities they serve are portrayed in a way that is true to form and truthful.

6.4. Considerations of an Ethical Nature

When dealing with cultural objects, particularly those that were obtained during times of colonial rule, ethical issues are an important factor to take into account. There is a possibility that questions regarding repatriation and reparations could surface, which will lead to difficult ethical conundrums.

The utilization of museums as a central component in cultural diplomacy is a powerful tool for fostering international ties and mutual understanding. It does this by fostering discussion, constructing bridges between states, and employing culture, art, and legacy as means to exert an influence on international relations. The advent of the internet age has given cultural diplomacy new dimensions, making cultural exchange easier to participate in and more widespread in its scope.

The potential for museums and other cultural institutions to promote global cooperation and mutual understanding through cultural diplomacy is enormous, despite the fact that there are still many obstacles and ethical considerations to take into account. Museums contribute to a more connected and harmonious world by highlighting the richness and diversity of human culture. This helps to break down boundaries and makes the world a better place overall.

Chapter 6

Museums and Community Engagement

The role of museums in society as organizations that preserve and display our collective history, art, and culture has been recognized for a long time as being particularly important. In spite of this, throughout the course of the past few decades, museums have initiated a process that will radically alter their function within local communities. More and more people regard museums not only as places to store artifacts and information, but also as vibrant hubs where members of the community can get involved in meaningful ways. This shift in perspective sheds light on the developing dynamic that exists between museums and the communities they serve by putting an emphasis on inclusivity, accessibility, and interaction. In the course of this all-encompassing investigation, we are going to dive into the significance of museums in community involvement, as well as their growing roles, the techniques that they apply, and the impact that they have on both individuals and communities.

1. **The Role of Museums as Engaging Agents in Their Communities**
   1.1. **How the Function of Museums Is Evolving**
   Throughout the course of human history, museums have traditionally been viewed as establishments that are primarily responsible for the acquisition, preservation, and display of cultural and historical items. Their major purpose was to act as stores of information, and they were frequently seen as locations where one could go for peaceful reflection and unaccompanied inquiry. The idea of a museum, on the other hand, has developed over the course of time, and as a result, museums play a more varied role in society today.
   In recent decades, museums have evolved from elitist institutions into community hubs that welcome all members of the local population. This shift is being brought about by the aspiration to make culture, art, history, and science available to a greater number of people, as opposed to only a chosen few. Museums are no longer unchanging locations; rather, they have evolved into vibrant hubs

that serve as centers for civic involvement, social interaction, and education. Their responsibilities now encompass a wider range of areas, including community involvement, the promotion of a sense of belonging, and the examination of modern challenges.

1.2. The Value of Participating in Community Activities

The term "community engagement" refers to the cooperation, involvement, and interaction that takes place between museums and the communities that they are tasked with serving. It involves actively soliciting input, listening to the needs and interests of the community, and working together to co-create museum experiences that are meaningful to the community. It is impossible to exaggerate how important it is for museums to foster active participation from the local community.

Community participation is the single most important factor in determining whether or not a museum will continue to serve its community's purpose and remain responsive to its shifting demographics and needs. It enables museums to attract visitors from a wider range of backgrounds, engage with members of underprivileged communities, and further the cause of social inclusion. Engaging the community not only helps to cultivate a sense of ownership and belonging, but it also helps to transform the museum into an important community resource. In addition to this, it has the potential to improve the whole visitor experience by rendering it more significant and personally relevant to individuals.

2. Methodologies for Productive Engagement with the Community

2.1. Collaborative Curation

Co-curation is one of the essential tactics that should be utilized for effective community engagement. Working together with people of the community to determine the content, design, and interpretation of exhibitions is what is meant by the term "co-curation." By taking this strategy, museums are able to incorporate a wide variety of viewpoints, voices, and tales. It helps dismantle the typical power dynamic that exists within museums, in which museum specialists decide what is displayed, and instead gives members of the community the authority to take a key role in the decision-making process.

The show "The Brooklyn Street Art" at the Brooklyn Museum is an excellent illustration of how co-curation may be done well. This show highlighted street art, a cultural phenomenon that has its origins deeply ingrained in the neighborhoods of Brooklyn. In order to put together the exhibit, the museum collaborated extensively with neighborhood residents, street artists, and community groups. The end product was a vivid and genuine illustration of the artistic expressions and social issues that are important to the community.

2.2. Programs Rooted in the Community

Creating programs that are rooted in the community is another productive technique for engaging with the people in the surrounding area.

Workshops, events, educational initiatives, and collaborative projects that directly include members of the community are examples of the kinds of programs that can fall under this category. By catering to the particular requirements and pursuits of their local communities, museums can establish themselves as reliable educational partners.

For example, the Cleveland Museum of Art started a program called "Studio Go" that offers art experiences directly to different areas all throughout the city. People are given the opportunity to make art, learn about the history of art, and engage with art in a setting that is easily accessible thanks to the establishment of mobile art studios in various areas. This program assures that art education and creative experiences are not restricted to the physical site of the museum, but rather that they may be enjoyed by various audiences in the neighborhoods where they live.

2.3. Sensitivity to Different Cultures and Accurate Portrayal

The importance of cultural awareness and representation cannot be overstated in relation to community participation. Museums have a responsibility to ensure that the cultural variety of the communities they serve is correctly reflected in their exhibitions and program offerings. It requires addressing historical biases as well as the legacy of colonialism and problems associated with cultural appropriation.

The National Museum of the American Indian in Washington, District of Columbia, is a fascinating example of cultural sensitivity. It may be found in the nation's capital. The Native American tribes are actively involved in the curatorial process at the museum, and the curators work closely with them to ensure that their cultures, history, and voices are appropriately reflected. They are challenging the preconceptions that are held about Native Americans and providing a forum for Native Americans to share their own experiences by doing so.

2.4. Participation in Digital Activities

The digital sphere is becoming an increasingly crucial instrument for museums to use in order to engage with the communities that surround them. The internet, social media, and virtual experiences all provide new channels that can be utilized to reach audiences who are increasingly numerous and varied. Through the use of digital platforms, museums are able to not only showcase their collections but also tell stories, offer instructional tools, and even solicit feedback from the local community.

The Rijksmuseum in Amsterdam is well-known for its innovative use of digital engagement, which has contributed to its success. They developed the digital platform known as "Rijksstudio," which gives users the ability to explore the huge contents of the museum, interact with those holdings, and even create their own collections using those holdings.

MUSEUMS AND GALLERIES

Through the use of this platform, the museum's resources are made available to an international audience, which encourages participation and the exchange of information.

3. **The Effects That Museums Have on Their Surrounding Communities**
   3.1. The Influence on Education
   The educational benefits that museums provide to the communities in which they are located are significant. They provide one-of-a-kind chances for hands-on learning, educational experiences, and immersive encounters with works of art, scientific research, and historical artifacts. Curiosity, critical thinking, and a love of learning are all encouraged by visits to museums.

   According to the findings of a research that was carried out by the American Alliance of Museums, museums are reliable sources of educational material; more than ninety-two percent of respondents believe that museums are essential for education. In addition, museums frequently form partnerships with schools in order to supply educational programs, field trips, and resources that serve the curriculum goals of the schools.

   3.2. Social Integration and Sense of Belonging
   It is essential for communities to have museums because they help strengthen social cohesiveness and promote inclusiveness. Museums create spaces for individuals of varying backgrounds to come together and interact by actively engaging with the populations in the communities in which they are located and representing a varied range of voices. This helps develop connections between diverse cultures and encourages understanding and tolerance among people of all backgrounds.

   For example, the Detroit Institute of Arts has participated in community engagement activities in order to advance the cause of inclusion. The museum has worked closely with community groups and artists in the area to develop exhibitions that are reflective of the cultural diversity that exists within the city. These efforts have helped to instill a sense of community pride and shared identity among the people who live in Detroit.

   3.3. The Effect on the Economy
   The local economies of the places where museums are located can be significantly impacted by their presence. They contribute to the economy of the area by attracting tourists, which in turn generates cash.

   When it comes to cultural tourism, museums are frequently one of the most important drivers, as they draw people who then spend money at local hotels, restaurants, and other businesses. In addition, museums generate employment possibilities, which is beneficial to the local labor force.

   For instance, not only is the Louvre Museum in Paris a symbol of the city's cultural heritage, but it is also a significant economic driver for the city. It brings in millions of visitors every year, which results in huge revenue for the city and the businesses located there. The economic advantages provided by museums are not limited to large establishments but also accrue to community-based museums and cultural groups of a smaller scale.

3.4. The Empowerment of the Community

Participation in community activities offered by museums can give local residents more agency. A sense of ownership and responsibility is instilled in communities whenever they are given the opportunity to actively participate in the decision-making processes of museums. This sense of empowerment has the potential to go beyond the walls of the museum and have an impact on broader social and political issues.

The Wing Luke Museum of the Asian Pacific American Experience in Seattle is a wonderful illustration of how communities can take control of their own narratives and histories. Exhibits and programming at the museum are frequently designed in conjunction with the Asian Pacific American population in the surrounding area. The museum has been able to not only tell the community's tales, but also give them the tools they need to advocate for their own rights and requirements because of their participation.

4. Obstacles and Factors to Consider When Engaging the Community in Museums

4.1. Restricted Access to Resources

Even though community engagement is crucial for museums, it frequently calls for a large investment of resources. Developing community-based programs, working in collaboration with local organizations, and putting digital engagement strategies into action can be challenging in terms of both finances and logistics. When it comes to properly connecting with their local communities, smaller museums or those with restricted funds may have more difficulty.

Museums can address the issue of limited resources by applying for grants, securing corporate sponsorships, and forming partnerships with other groups.

Additionally, they should make inclusivity and diversity in their staffing a priority in order to guarantee that their teams accurately reflect the communities that they serve, which can result in engagement activities that are more successful and culturally sensitive.

4.2. Obstacles Presented by Change

It's possible that museum professionals and other stakeholders will push back against changes that are tied to community engagement. There is a possibility that traditional methods of curation and exhibition design are strongly ingrained in the culture of the institution. Some people may view the transition toward community-based decision-making at the museum with suspicion or hostility because they believe it puts the institution's credibility or expertise at risk.

To overcome resistance to change in a company, it is necessary to make changes in both the culture and the leadership of the business. It is important for museums to encourage a culture that values flexibility and lifelong education. Staff members and stakeholders can have a better understanding of the benefits of community engagement and how it ties in with the goal of the museum by participating in training and education programs.

4.3. Striking a Balance Between Innovation and Tradition

It is necessary for museums to strike a balance between their more conventional duties as the keepers of cultural artifacts and their changing roles as the centers of community interaction. It is not always simple to strike this balance, since there can be friction between the preservation of legacy and the promotion of new projects that are driven by the community.

The "Museum of the Future" initiative being undertaken by the British Museum is one example of an endeavor to strike a balance between innovation and tradition. It requires reinventing both the physical space and the digital offerings of the museum, all while ensuring that the museum continues to fulfill its primary purpose of storing and exhibiting historical items. Obtaining this equilibrium is a never-ending challenge that calls for careful planning and collaborative discussion.

4.4. Discussing Content That May Be Controversial Or Sensitive

It's possible that participating in community engagement activities at museums will require discussing touchy or divisive subjects, such as colonialism, social justice, or political history. The community may be divided along a number of lines and experience a range of intense feelings as a result of these challenges, making it difficult to find common ground and a solution.

These problems have been effectively addressed by the National Museum of African American History and Culture in Washington, District of Columbia, which creates an environment that is welcoming, respectful, and safe for conversation and introspection.

They have produced programs and exhibitions that enable conversations about race, identity, and social justice within their community, which has helped to foster understanding and empathy among its members.

The transformation of museums into hubs for community participation is an encouraging sign for the future of our country's cultural and educational institutions. Museums are evolving into venues that are active, dynamic, and welcoming to all visitors; they are no longer static institutions. They provide a variety of communities with access to knowledge, inspiration, and connections between one another.

Co-curation, community-based activities, cultural sensitivity, and digital engagement are some of the tactics for effective community involvement that museums may utilize as powerful instruments to guarantee that they continue to be relevant and responsive to the needs and interests of their respective communities. The educational, social, economic, and empowering benefits that museums provide to the communities in which they are located are clear indicators of the influence that museums have.

However, museums are also subject to a number of obstacles, such as limited access to resources, reluctance to change, the requirement to strike a balance between tradition and innovation, and the discussion of touchy subjects. In order to prevail over these obstacles, you will need to demonstrate a dedication to adaptation, diversity, and thoughtful leadership.

6.1 Museums as community hubs

The traditional conception of museums as unchanging receptacles for historical relics and works of art has been replaced by a newer, more dynamic conception in recent years. conventional institutions have transformed into crucial community hubs that serve as essential centers for cultural engagement, educational opportunities, and social interaction. These community hubs have evolved from conventional institutions. Museums now actively strive to build connections within their communities, operating not only as institutions that preserve the past but also actively impact the present and the future. Embracing a strategy that is more inclusive and participatory, museums now actively seek to foster connections within their communities. In this essay, we will look into the multidimensional role that museums play as community hubs, investigating their growing purposes, the impact they have on local communities, and the tactics that museums utilize to effectively engage with their different audiences.

Shifting Focuses and Functions of Museums

The traditional function of museums as keepers of cultural history has evolved to include a more proactive engagement with the communities in which they are located. Museums nowadays are not content to merely display historical relics; rather, they strive to become dynamic community spaces that represent the diversity and depth of the communities in which they are located.

They want to be more approachable and inclusive, accepting people from a wide range of ethnicities and backgrounds in the hopes of generating a sense of belonging and ownership among members of the community. This transition is illustrative of a larger cultural trend toward more community involvement and collaboration in a variety of areas of public life, and it reflects the importance of these developments.

Creating Opportunities for Intercultural Communication and Understanding

The promotion of intercultural communication and understanding is one of the most important functions that museums do in their capacity as community hubs. Museums provide a venue for intercultural interaction and the cultivation of mutual respect by displaying a wide range of artistic practices, historical narratives, and cultural practices. The cultural legacy of various communities is frequently honored through exhibitions and events, and attendees are encouraged to investigate and gain a better understanding of the customs and behaviors of those from other communities. This encourages cultural awareness and helps to develop a community that is more accepting and tolerant of differences, one in which different communities may coexist peacefully and understand the distinctive identities of one another.

Education and Continued Professional Development

Museums have developed into important educational institutions in recent years, providing one-of-a-kind and immersive educational opportunities for visitors of all ages. Museums encourage a passion of learning that lasts a lifetime by providing a variety of learning opportunities, including hands-on workshops, instructional events, and interactive exhibitions. They offer educational tools that are designed to supplement conventional schooling, making it possible for visitors to engage with a variety of topics in a manner that is hands-on and experiential. Museums ensure that education is not limited to the confines of the classroom by embracing interactive technologies and new learning approaches. Instead, museums ensure that education extends into the dynamic and engaging environments they provide for the communities they serve.

Increasing Social Cohesion While Maintaining an Inclusive Attitude

Museums, which often act as community hubs, can play a catalytic role in the promotion of social cohesion and inclusivity. Museums contribute to the growth of a society that is more equitable and just when they actively engage with underserved populations and address social issues. Museums make it possible for people from all walks of life to engage in cultural activities and have access to materials that would otherwise be out of their reach by implementing outreach programs and projects that are specifically tailored to their audiences. This inclusivity helps to build a sense of social belonging and empowers marginalized groups, which contributes to the bridging of social gaps and the promotion of a society that is more cohesive and united.

Promoting Participation in Civic Life and Conversation

Museums frequently play the role of platforms for civic participation and public conversation, providing locations in which people of the community can congregate to discuss urgent topics and share their points of view. Museums stimulate conversation on issues of regional, national, and international significance by hosting public debates, lectures, and community-driven events on a regular basis. These projects not only encourage residents to participate actively in their communities, but they also instill a feeling of collective responsibility and provide community members more agency. Museums provide a significant contribution to the creation of informed and engaged communities that are actively involved in determining their shared future by acting as a forum for debates that are both open and productive.

Strategies for Efficient Participation in Community Activities

In order for museums to fulfill their role as community hubs in an efficient manner, they must implement a number of tactics targeted at creating meaningful connections with its audience members. These tactics include community-based curating, which is when members of the community actively participate in the selection and interpretation of exhibitions. This helps to ensure that the narratives presented are consistent with the experiences that the local population has really had. To actively engage with a variety of groups and to generate chances for social contact and cultural exchange, museums often host community-centered events and activities such as cultural festivals, workshops, and outreach efforts. In addition, museums are now able to reach a wider audience and encourage participation from people all over the world in their community-oriented programs by incorporating digital engagement into their operations in the form of online exhibitions, virtual tours, and interactive platforms.

Conquering Obstacles While Keeping an Eye on the Future

Despite the fact that they play increasingly important roles in their communities, museums as community hubs confront a number of obstacles in their efforts to cultivate meaningful relationships and involvement among members of the communities they serve. There are major obstacles that museum workers face, including limited financial resources, shifting visitor expectations, and the requirement to strike a balance between preservation and community participation. In addition, the ongoing digital revolution and the need to adapt to fast changing technology necessitate museums to consistently innovate and develop new methods to effectively connect and engage with their audiences. This is because the digital revolution is expected to continue for the foreseeable future. Nevertheless, museums may overcome these problems and continue to function as lively and dynamic community hubs that inspire, educate, and connect diverse people if they form strategic alliances, develop new programming, and make a commitment to community-centered initiatives.

Museums have evolved from inert storage facilities for artifacts into dynamic and welcoming community hubs that celebrate diversity, encourage education, and advance social harmony. Museums play an essential part in the development of thriving and connected communities by recognizing and embracing the role that they serve as cultural and educational organizations. Because of their dedication to community participation, museums continue to play an important role as hubs for the sharing of cultural ideas, the pursuit of lifelong learning, and the facilitation of social empowerment, all of which enrich the lives of individuals as well as communities. Museums will surely continue to be vital foundations of cultural enrichment and social growth within their communities as they continue to adapt and innovate in response to shifting societal needs and advancements in technology.

6.2 Outreach programs and initiatives

The development of social and community resources, such as outreach programs and initiatives, is an indispensable part of the process. These initiatives work as bridges that connect corporations, institutions, and individuals with the communities that they intend to positively influence for the better. Outreach projects, whether they are motivated by educational, social, or humanitarian goals, play an important role in resolving a variety of difficulties, creating inclusivity, and bringing about significant change. During this in-depth investigation, we are going to delve into the realm of outreach programs and initiatives, investigating their relevance, the various domains

MUSEUMS AND GALLERIES

that they cover, the techniques that they apply, and the significant impact that they have on both individuals and communities.

1. **The Importance of Different Types of Community Outreach Programs and Initiatives**
   1.1. Meeting the Requirements of the Community
   The many outreach programs and initiatives are adapted to cater to the particular requirements of the communities they serve. These requirements can include a wide variety of topics, such as education, healthcare, poverty, social justice, and perhaps more. These initiatives frequently act as crucial safety nets for populations that are underserved or vulnerable, filling the gaps left by other groups or by the government in terms of service provision. Outreach programs serve a significant role in improving the quality of life for people who, in the absence of support, may otherwise be left without assistance. These programs do this by actively identifying and addressing the needs of the community.
   1.2. Fostering an Attitude of Inclusivity
   The principle of inclusivity underlies all of the many outreach programs and activities. These programs frequently concentrate on underserved or underrepresented populations, with the goal of ensuring that those who are at the greatest risk of being harmed or falling further behind have access to the resources, opportunities, and support that they require. persons who are a member of these groups need to be given the ability to engage actively in societal processes and decision-making so that inclusivity isn't just about giving resources but also about empowering those persons.
   1.3. Creating More Self-Determination
   Empowerment of individuals and communities is a primary focus of many of the outreach initiatives that are offered. These programs assist individuals in acquiring the information and capabilities essential to overcoming obstacles and bettering their lives by making resources, education, and assistance more readily available to them. Individuals should not just have their immediate needs met in order to be empowered; rather, they should also be provided with the resources necessary to become self-sufficient, assume control of their situations, and make decisions based on accurate information.
   1.4. Fourteenth Point: Strengthening Community Resilience
   The capacity of a community to endure and recover from shocks and stresses, such as those caused by natural catastrophes, economic crises, or public health emergencies, is referred to as community resilience. The provision of support, education, and resources that assist communities in preparing for and reacting to problems is facilitated by outreach programs and initiatives, which play a vital part in the building of resilience within communities. These initiatives frequently entail emergency preparedness, financial literacy, access to healthcare,

and other aspects that contribute to a community's capacity to rebound after experiencing adversity.

2. **The Wide-Ranging Subject Matters That Can Be Approached Through Outreach Programs and Initiatives**

2.1. Schooling/Education

The goal of education outreach programs is to provide access to high-quality education, particularly for communities that are not currently being serviced. After-school programs, scholarships, tutoring, and mentoring are some examples of the many different guises that these projects might take. They frequently focus on the children and adolescents living in disadvantaged communities, assisting them in overcoming the obstacles that stand in the way of their educational success. In order to combat educational disparities and enable students to realize their full potential, initiatives such as "Teach for America" and "Girls Who Code" have been developed.

2.2. The Healthcare System

People who may not have proper access to medical services, health education, and preventative care are the primary target audience for healthcare outreach initiatives, which focus on providing these individuals with these opportunities. Among these activities may be mobile clinics, vaccination campaigns, information programs for the general population, and other initiatives designed to combat particular diseases or disorders.

Both "Doctors Without Borders" and the "Red Cross" are well-known organizations that provide humanitarian aid in the form of healthcare outreach programs in an effort to reduce human suffering and enhance public health.

2.3. Justice in Social Situations

Those who work in the field of social justice develop outreach initiatives with the goal of combating systematic discrimination, inequality, and injustice. They frequently try to modify policies and practices that are the root cause of these problems, all while offering support to individuals who have been negatively impacted by them. Examples of groups that engage in outreach initiatives centered on social justice include organizations with names like the "American Civil Liberties Union" (ACLU) and the "National Association for the Advancement of Colored People" (NAACP).

2.4. Reduction of the Effects of Poverty

Initiatives aimed at reducing economic inequities and offering assistance to individuals and families already living in poverty are referred to as "poverty alleviation." Training in financial literacy, microfinance, job training, and food banks are some examples of the kind of programs that fall under this category. Both "Grameen Bank" and "Habitat for Humanity" are well-known throughout the world for the outreach activities they do in an effort to fight against poverty.

2.5. Protection of the Natural Environment

The goals of outreach initiatives in environmental conservation are to increase knowledge about environmental challenges, encourage sustainable behaviors, and engage communities in efforts to conserve the environment. Quite frequently, they include activities such as educational campaigns, community clean-up days, and projects focused at safeguarding natural ecosystems. Organizations such as "The Nature Conservancy" and "Greenpeace" are two examples of groups that participate in outreach initiatives that are related to the conservation of the environment.

2.6. Art and Cultural Activities

The goal of outreach initiatives in the arts and culture sector is to broaden participation in artistic and cultural activities among all members of a community. Free or cheap admission to museums, cultural festivals, art workshops, and programs that promote local artists are all examples of what might be included in these types of initiatives. Both the "Smithsonian Institution" and "Artreach" have garnered acclaim for the significant contributions they have made toward broadening people's access to the arts and culture.

3. Methodologies Utilized in Community Involvement Programs and Initiatives

3.1. An Analysis of Your Requirements

It is common practice for companies to carry out exhaustive needs assessments before beginning outreach program development. In the course of these evaluations, we collect data, carry out surveys, and interact with members of the community in order to identify particular requirements, obstacles, and priorities. It is absolutely necessary to have a solid understanding of the specific environment of a community in order to successfully customize programs.

3.2. Participation in the Community

The active participation of the communities that are served is given the utmost importance in

effective outreach programs. Building relationships with community people, paying attention to what they have to say, and including them in the decision-making process are all aspects of this involvement. It ensures that programs are sensitive to the local culture, responsive to the preferences of the community, and actually address the requirements of the community as a whole.

3.3. Relationships With Others

When it comes to outreach programs, collaborative alliances are absolutely necessary. In the context of these collaborations, collaboration with local organizations, government agencies, nonprofit organizations, and community leaders is frequently required in order to maximize the utilization of resources, expertise, and support. Organizations are able to broaden their reach and have a greater overall impact on the world when they work together with a variety of stakeholders.

3.4. Awareness and Educational Initiatives

In many different outreach efforts, education and increasing levels of awareness are essential techniques. Whether the goal of the program is to advocate for social justice, raise awareness about environmental issues, or promote health education, these programs frequently feature educational campaigns, seminars, and events that inform and engage the local community.

3.5. Participant Autonomy and Enhanced Skill Development

The concept of self-determination is at the heart of many different types of outreach programs. The participants in these programs are provided with the education, training, and tools necessary for them to regain control of their life and make significant strides toward achieving their goals. The cultivation of skills, the training of financial literacy, and the participation in vocational programs are typical components of these initiatives.

3.6. Monitoring and Evaluation

It is vital to monitor and evaluate outreach activities on a regular basis in order to accurately measure their impact and level of efficacy. Frequently, organizations will outline their goals in detail and make use of measurable indicators to monitor their progress. Organizations are able to better serve the areas they are responsible for by continually analyzing their programs and making any required adjustments and enhancements.

4. An Analysis of the Effects Produced by Outreach Programs and Initiatives

4.1. Enhancing One's Existence and Quality of Life

Individuals and communities can expect to see a direct and measurable improvement in their overall quality of life as a result of participation in outreach activities. These programs enable people to lead lives that are healthier and more meaningful by addressing a variety of needs. These needs include healthcare, education, and social assistance, among others. It is common for improvements in well-being, economic security, and personal development to follow after gaining access to high-quality education, healthcare services, and social assistance.

4.2. Mitigating the Effects of Inequality

The reduction of inequality within communities is significantly aided by the implementation of outreach programs. They work to level the playing field by giving people who may have fallen behind owing to a variety of disadvantages the opportunity and resources they need to catch up with the rest of the pack. These programs help to a more equitable society by addressing the inequities that are embedded in the system as a whole and by offering assistance to groups on the margins of society.

4.3. Promoting the Cohesion of the Community

Community cohesion and a sense of belonging are fostered through the implementation of outreach activities. They frequently get members of the community involved in projects and activities that stimulate connection, collaboration, and the exchange of experiences. This helps to cultivate a sense of oneness among the community and reinforces the social relationships that already exist there.

4.4. Develop Your Capacity for Resilience

Outreach activities are an essential component in the process of constructing resilient communities. These efforts equip communities to resist shocks and adapt to changing conditions. Whether they focus on preparedness for natural disasters, economic stability, or health education, these projects empower communities. Communities that are resilient are better able to bounce back after experiencing hardship and thrive in spite of the obstacles they confront.

4.5. Facilitating Social Transformation

The promotion of social transformation is one of the many goals of the numerous outreach programs that are currently available. These initiatives contribute to the transformation of wider societal structures and practices by addressing problems at the systemic level and pushing for changes in policy. They frequently serve as the impetus for wider social movements and general advancement.

4.6. Providing Independence to Individuals

The empowerment of individuals is one of the most significant effects that may be brought about by outreach activities. These programs assist individuals in acquiring the information, capabilities, and self-assurance necessary to take charge of their own life. This empowerment typically results in increased self-esteem, personal development, and the capacity to advocate for oneself and one's communities.

5. Obstacles and Things to Think About When Designing Outreach Programs and Initiatives

5.1. Restricted Access to Resources

The availability of resources is frequently an issue for outreach efforts, which can restrict both their reach and their impact. It may not always be possible to provide services and support in an efficient manner due to factors such as limited funding and staffing, staffing shortages, and logistical issues. To overcome these limitations will require innovative fundraising strategies, effective utilization of available resources, and close cooperation with other organizations.

5.2. Sensitivity to Other Cultures

Given the variety and individuality of the populations being served by outreach initiatives, cultural awareness is of the utmost importance. It is crucial to success to implement programs that respect the cultural norms, customs, and beliefs of different groups. In the absence of cultural awareness, initiatives run the risk of accidentally isolating or harming the very communities that they intend to assist.

5.3. Long-Term Viability

Numerous outreach programs are concerned about their ability to remain sustainable. It is often necessary for these projects to shift their focus from giving immediate relief to supporting long-term growth and self-sufficiency in order for them to have an impact that is long-lasting. In order to guarantee the long-term viability of programs, it is necessary to engage in rigorous planning and capacity building, as well as to place an emphasis on empowering both individuals and communities.

5.4. Obstacles in the Political and Social Domains

There is a possibility that outreach programs could face political and social opposition, which will have an effect on their operations. It may be difficult to deliver services or advocate for change due to barriers posed by policies enacted by the government, social resistance, and competing interests. In order to overcome these obstacles, it is often necessary to engage in strategic advocacy, community mobilization, and the formation of coalitions.

5.5. The Analysis of the Impact

It might be difficult to determine how effective certain outreach campaigns are. In many cases, sophisticated monitoring and evaluation mechanisms are required in order to ascertain whether or not programs are successful in attaining their intended results and in positively impacting the lives of members of the community. It is vital to collect and analyze data in order to measure impact, yet doing so can require a significant amount of resources.

5.6. Considerations of an Ethical Nature

When it comes to outreach projects, ethical considerations are of the utmost importance, particularly when working with vulnerable or marginalized populations. The upholding of ethical values, the valuing of human autonomy and rights, and the guaranteeing of the dignity and well-being of those who are served are all key factors in the design and execution of programs.

The implementation of various outreach programs and initiatives is a crucial part of the process of bringing about good change in communities. These initiatives are aimed at addressing particular needs, fostering an inclusive environment, and providing individuals and communities with the tools necessary to improve their quality of life. These programs have a significant effect on quality of life, inequality, community cohesiveness, and resilience as a result of their engagement with a wide variety of communities and their utilization of a wide range of tactics. They play an important role in creating social change and enabling individuals to develop the skills necessary to become self-sufficient and engaged members of the communities in which they live. The importance of outreach programs in developing a more just and equal society cannot be emphasized, despite the fact that there are obstacles and factors to take into consideration. Their part in constructing a better and more welcoming future is an essential one, and it will continue to develop as they adjust to the shifting requirements of the community and the dynamics of society.

6.3 Collaborations with local communities

Multiple programs in the governmental sector, the business sector, and the nonprofit sector all rely heavily on collaborative efforts with the communities in their respective areas. These partnerships, which are motivated by the realization of the cumulative power of community involvement, have the ability to bring about positive change on a variety of different fronts. Collaborative efforts with local communities play a vital role in addressing difficult challenges and attaining shared goals, whether the context is urban development, healthcare, education, environmental conservation, or social justice. This is true whether the focus is on urban development, healthcare, education, environmental conservation, or social justice. In the course of this in-depth investigation, we will investigate the significance of working in conjunction with the communities that are located in a certain area, as well as the many different fields in which such collaborations are utilized, the methods that can be utilized to ensure productive participation, and the significant effects that such collaborations can have on both the communities and the organizations that are engaged.

1. **The Significance of Working Together with Neighborhoods and Communities**
   1.1. Community-Based Approaches to Problem Solving
   Collaborations with local communities are founded on the principle that the people who live in a certain region are in the best position to comprehend the particular difficulties and requirements of that region. These partnerships aim to generate solutions that are not only pertinent but also effective in addressing the problem at hand. It is possible for organizations to tailor their programs, policies, and initiatives to address issues directly from the perspective of those who are most affected by them if they involve community members in the decision-making process and involve community members in the decision-making process.
   1.2. Integrity of Participation and Representation
   When people from different backgrounds work together on a local level, they increase the likelihood that their perspectives will be taken into account throughout the decision-making process. This inclusiveness is absolutely necessary in order to construct a society that is more egalitarian. These relationships encourage a feeling of ownership and belonging within the community by actively interacting with a diverse variety of individuals of the community. This helps to ensure that the requirements of underserved or marginalized communities are not neglected.
   1.3. Empowerment at the Grassroots
   Individuals and groups are given the ability to be active agents of change through the process of collaborating with local communities. Members of the community are better able to advocate for their rights, gain access to resources, and bring about positive change in their own communities if they collaborate and work together.
   This empowerment extends beyond the immediate goals of a cooperation and

contributes to the long-term self-sufficiency and resilience of communities. This empowerment goes beyond the immediate goals of a collaboration.

1.4. Developing and Maintaining Social Capital

The term "social capital," which refers to the relationships, trust, and networks that exist inside communities, is cultivated through partnerships with local communities. These relationships are extremely helpful in times of crisis, in assisting with the growth of the community, in fostering group cohesiveness and in providing mutual support. Through the building of ties between residents, organizations, and local leaders, social capital can be increased through collaborative efforts.

2. **Types of Partnerships with Neighborhood and Community Organizations**

2.1. Urban Development and Neighborhood Revitalization

Collaborations with existing communities are an absolutely necessary component of urban planning and development. The initiatives include both community-led design and placemaking efforts, in addition to neighborhood redevelopment projects and the building of affordable housing. Participation from the local community in urban development projects helps to ensure that those initiatives are tailored to the requirements and preferences of the community. This, in turn, contributes to the improvement of people' quality of life.

2.2. Healthcare and the General Population's Health

Collaborations amongst members of the community are absolutely necessary in the field of healthcare in order to advance public health, access to healthcare, and preventative measures. Outreach activities, community health clinics, health education campaigns, and partnerships with local organizations are all examples of what can fall under this category. The discrepancies in medical care are one of the issues that will hopefully be addressed through these collaborations, as is the overall health of the community's residents.

2.3. Educational Opportunities and the Progress of Young People

The primary goal of educational partnerships with local communities is to enhance the educational opportunities available to children, particularly in regions that are currently underserved. Mentorship, after-school activities, parental involvement, and community schools are all possible components of these programs. These programs are intended to help children and young people improve in all aspects of their development, including their academic performance.

2.4. Protection of the Natural Environment

Local partnerships are essential to the success of environmental conservation efforts because they help preserve natural ecosystems, lessen the impact on the environment, and advance sustainable practices. Planting trees, reducing waste, protecting wildlife, and participating in educational programs that encourage ecologically responsible habits are all examples of possible community partnership activities. Participation from local communities is essential to the accomplishment of conservation objectives and the cultivation of a feeling of environmental responsibility.

2.5. The Role of Advocacy and Social Justice

In the pursuit of social justice and activism, the importance of collaborations with local communities cannot be overstated. These projects are working to tackle inequality, prejudice, and injustice that are embedded in the system. Partnerships frequently involve organizing at the grassroots level, advocating for specific policies, and conducting public awareness campaigns in order to combat unfair practices and advance fairness.

2.6. Art and Cultural Activities

Collaborations with local communities help to deliver a variety of cultural experiences to a wide range of audiences in the field of arts and culture. Community art projects, cultural festivals, and other types of efforts that bring together people and local artists may be included in some programs. The cultural fabric of neighborhoods is enriched as a result of these collaborations, and more people are inspired to participate in artistic expression as a result.

3. Methods for Productive Cooperation with Neighborhood Communities

3.1. Taking Part in the Conversation

Active listening is the foundation of every successful collaboration. Engaging with local communities, gaining an understanding of their concerns, and showing respect for the insights they provide is required of organizations. The viewpoints and priorities of community members should be listened to in order to guarantee that the partnership will be motivated by a true grasp of their requirements.

3.2. Co-Creation

Participation of community members in the decision-making process is an essential part of the co-creation process. This method encourages a sense of ownership as well as shared accountability for the projects or activities that are being carried out. Participants from the local community are given equal roles in defining and carrying out the objectives of the cooperation.

3.3. Collaborations, Alliances, and Partnerships

For effective collaboration, forming ties with local organizations, community leaders, and community groups is crucial. These partnerships frequently expand the scope of the collaboration in terms of both its reach and its resources, thereby capitalizing on the experience and networks of local stakeholders.

3.4. Expanding Our Capabilities

The capacity of community members ought to be the primary emphasis of any collaborative efforts. This includes providing individuals and groups with the training, tools, and opportunity to develop the skills and knowledge essential for active participation and leadership roles.

3.5. Communication That Is Clear

In order for collaborative efforts to be successful, communication must be open and honest. It guarantees that members of the community are kept informed about the aims, progress, and results of the partnership. Trust and participation in activities can be increased through effective communication.

3.6. Adaptability to Change

It is important for collaborations to be adaptable and versatile in order to meet the ever-changing requirements of communities. The ability to be flexible grants organizations the ability to alter their strategies and operations so that they are in line with the evolving circumstances and priorities of the company.

4. The Effects of Partnerships with Neighborhood Groups and Communities

4.1. An Increased Satisfaction with Life

Collaborations with local communities almost always result in an improvement in the citizens' overall quality of life. These collaborations address crucial challenges and provide resources and support that promote the well-being of individuals and families. These issues can be addressed through urban development projects, healthcare efforts, or social justice campaigns.

4.2. The Empowerment of the Community

Individuals and groups are given the ability to exert more agency when they participate in collaborative efforts. This empowerment is not only helpful in overcoming current obstacles, but it is also essential in developing long-term self-sufficiency and resiliency. Members of the community take an active role in effecting change, fighting for their own rights and working to advance their own interests.

4.3. Fair and Equitable Results

Collaborations aim to achieve more equal results by narrowing the gaps between participants and fostering an inclusive environment. These efforts seek to level the playing field and guarantee that all members of the community have access to opportunities and resources by including members of underserved or underrepresented communities in the decision-making processes.

4.4. The Role of Social Capital

Through the cultivation of relationships and networks among residents, social capital can be grown within communities through the use of collaborative efforts. These social links contribute to the resilience and cohesion of communities, as well as their capacity to successfully respond to difficulties and catastrophes.

4.5. The Development of a Sustainable Environment

Collaborations with local communities can have a significant and positive impact on sustainable development. Frequently, the focus of these cooperation is on long-term solutions that address not only present requirements but also bigger difficulties. Collaborations provide a contribution to the continued development of communities by increasing their capacity and encouraging them to become more self-sufficient.

4.6. Promotion of Social Reform and Advocacy

Changes in policy and broader societal shifts are frequently the results of collaborative efforts in the fields of social justice and advocacy. These projects become catalysts for social change that reach beyond the boundaries of local communities because they target and work to eliminate fundamental disparities and promote fairness.

5. Obstacles and Factors to Consider When Working Together with Local Communities

5.1. Developing Trust in Others

It can be difficult to rebuild trust between organizations and people of the community, particularly in circumstances when such trust has been destroyed as a result of previous experiences or systemic problems. It is generally necessary to communicate in an open and honest manner, to consistently follow through, and to make a long-term commitment to working together in order to be successful in overcoming this obstacle.

5.2. Sensitivity to Other Cultures

When working together, having cultural awareness and sensitivity is of the utmost importance, especially in areas with a diverse population. To guarantee that their programs and activities are respectful and relevant to the community, organizations need to have a strong awareness of the cultural norms, values, and traditions that make up the community. Lack of sensitivity might result in misunderstandings and pushback from others.

5.3. Distribution of Available Resources

In the context of collaborations, resource allocation is a crucial factor because organizations frequently confront financial limits. It is important to provide careful consideration to decision-making on resource allocation in order to maximize the positive impact of the collaboration in a manner that is equal and fair.

5.4. Coordination and Administrative and Supervisory Roles

It is absolutely necessary to have strong leadership and good coordination in order for collaborations to be successful. The importance of having well-defined roles, duties, and communication systems cannot be overstated. It is a difficult undertaking that requires strong leadership that must be accomplished in order to guarantee that all partners are aligned with the goals and activities of the partnership.

5.5. Long-Term Viability

In many different kinds of partnerships, maintaining the relationship is difficult. It is necessary to engage in meticulous planning and capacity-building in order to guarantee that the benefits gained from the collaboration will be long-lasting and self-sustaining. In order for programs to have a positive impact over the long term, they should focus on empowering individuals of the community and helping them grow their skills and resources.

5.6. Considerations of an Ethical Nature

When working in conjunction with local communities, ethical issues are of the utmost importance. The upholding of ethical standards, the respecting of the autonomy and rights of individuals, and the guaranteeing of the dignity and well-being of members of the community are all key factors in the design and implementation of programs.

Strong, effective vehicles for bringing about positive change and tackling difficult difficulties can be found in the form of collaborative efforts with local communities. These relationships encourage the development of community-centered solutions, inclusivity, and empowerment, as well as the cultivation of social capital. They have a significant influence on the quality of life of inhabitants, helping to eliminate inequality, bolstering resiliency, and promoting social reform. The key to productive collaboration is the use of effective tactics, such as active listening, co-creation, partnerships, and clear communication.

The importance of these collaborations in developing more egalitarian and empowered communities cannot be emphasized, despite the fact that there are hurdles and factors to take into account. Their contribution to the development of a better and more welcoming future is absolutely essential, and the extent to which they are able to effect good change is continuously expanding as they learn to accommodate the shifting requirements and dynamics of the communities in which they operate.

Chapter 7

Technological Advancements in Museums

Although museums have traditionally played the role of preserving cultural heritage, historical information, and artistic works, the function that museums perform in society has changed substantially over the course of human history. In this day and age, museums are embracing technological innovations in order to improve the experiences they provide for visitors, increase their audience, and strengthen their efforts to preserve cultural artifacts. This essay investigates the significant influence that technology has had on museums, diving into the myriad of ways in which it has altered the appearance of both traditional and virtual museum spaces. The advent of new technologies has ushered in a new era for museums, ushering in everything from augmented reality to fully immersive exhibits, as well as the digitalization of collections and interactive instructional aids.

1. **A General Introduction to Recent Technological Developments in Museums Enhanced Visitor Experiences:** Modern technology provides new tools and interactive elements that can engage visitors in fresh and engaging ways, so increasing their comprehension of and appreciation for museum exhibitions.
   Preserving Digital Artifacts and Objects Museums are rapidly digitizing their collections in order to make them available to audiences all over the world while also protecting fragile artifacts and works of art.
   Tools for Education Educational technology is being used to help assist learning and provide context for museum displays in order to appeal to a wide variety of visitors, including students and people who continue to study throughout their lives.
   The concept of accessibility is being reimagined because to the rise of online and virtual museums, which make it possible for people all over the world to remotely experience cultural heritage and art collections.
   The preservation of relics, as well as their restoration and conservation, are made

easier with the help of modern technology, which ensures that these artifacts will be around for future generations to enjoy.

Data Analysis and Interpretation: Museums are utilizing data analytics and interpretation tools to obtain insights about the behavior of visitors, the preferences of visitors, and the success of exhibits.

2. **Increasing the Quality of the Experiences of Visitors**

   Both Augmented Reality (AR) and Virtual Reality (VR) are types of mixed reality

   The augmented reality (AR) and virtual reality (VR) technologies allow users to have immersive experiences by superimposing digital information over the real world or by building wholly virtual worlds. AR and VR are being used in museums to create interactive exhibitions that let visitors explore historical scenes, step inside artworks, and mimic archaeological digs.

   For example, the Cleveland Museum of Art has launched a mobile app that features augmented reality in order to improve the experience of museum visitors. The app provides users with a number of interactive features, such as a virtual guide, that change based on where the user is physically located within the museum.

   Exhibits That Encourage Interaction

   Touchscreens, sensors, and other forms of technology are used in interactive displays so that visitors are encouraged to participate. These exhibitions provide guests with the opportunity to investigate a variety of topics, engage in the manipulation of digital content, and develop a more profound comprehension of the subject matter. Interactive displays can be found in museums such as the Exploratorium in San Francisco, which invite visitors to get their hands dirty while learning about scientific principles.

   Audio Tours and Mobile Applications

   Technology has completely altered the experience of using audio guides in museums. Audio tours of modern museums frequently take the form of apps for smartphones, and they offer visitors a plethora of information about the exhibits, such as audio explanations, historical context, and supplementary multimedia content. The use of these apps provides users with a tailored experience by letting them select the content that is most pertinent to their particular areas of interest. One example is the mobile app that the Louvre Museum in Paris provides, which includes in-depth audio guides for the museum's extensive collection.

   The use of Quick Response (QR) Codes and Near Field Communication (NFC)

   QR codes and other forms of near-field communication (NFC) technology are used to give visitors rapid access to supplementary information about artworks and exhibits. Visitors are able to instantly access multimedia information, extensive descriptions, and historical context by scanning QR codes or utilizing devices that are enabled with NFC technology. Visitors to the Smithsonian National Museum of American History can gain access to more in-depth information regarding the artifacts that are on display by scanning QR codes.

The process of gaming

Gamification is utilized at museums to pique the interest of visitors, particularly younger audiences. Elements of gamification like treasure hunts, quizzes, and other challenges stimulate active engagement and learning. For instance, the National Gallery in London provides families who come to the museum with the opportunity to participate in a treasure hunt game, which makes the visit both entertaining and informative.

3. **The Conservation of Digital Assets**

    The Process of Digitizing Collections

    The digitization of museum collections is becoming increasingly common as an approach for preserving delicate items and making them available to audiences all over the world. In order to generate digital copies of historical artifacts and works of art, high-resolution imaging, three-dimensional scanning, and virtual tours are utilized. This digitizing initiative not only protects the physical artifacts but also makes it easier to conduct research and reach out to the educational community.

    The British Museum, which is one of the most well-known and largest museums in the world, possesses a sizable digital collection that includes photographs of exceptionally high quality as well as 3D models of various items. The general public, academics, and educators all have access to these digital tools, which make it possible to conduct in-depth investigations of the museum's collections.

    Archive and Database Services Available Online

    Online archives and databases containing extensive information about a museum's collection are frequently updated and maintained by museums. Researchers, students, and members of the general public are all able to access historical documents, pictures, and scholarly information that is associated with museum collections thanks to these tools. For example, the Smithsonian Institution has a large online database that contains entries for millions of artifacts housed in its many museums and research institutes.

    Content Generated by the Crowd

    The public is invited to participate in the digitization process by some museums through the use of crowdsourcing projects. Volunteers can assist with the identification of objects, the transcription of historical documents, and the addition of information to digital resources. The "What's on the Menu?" project run by the New York Public Library is an excellent illustration of crowdsourcing. In this initiative, volunteers transcribe historical restaurant menus in order to make them searchable and accessible.

4. **Materials for Instruction**
   Platforms for Digital Instruction
   Museums are currently developing digital learning platforms and materials in order to broaden the range of educational opportunities available to its visitors. These systems make it easier for teachers and students to access museum content by providing lesson plans, films, interactive activities, and virtual field excursions. For example, the Metropolitan Museum of Art in New York provides K-12 teachers with access to a vast array of educational tools and course materials. The museum is located in Central Park.
   Classes and Seminars Conducted Online
   Participants are given the opportunity to explore further into art, history, science, and culture through the participation in online courses and workshops offered by many museums. These classes typically cater to students who continue their education throughout their lives and provide an environment that encourages independent study at the student's own pace. The Museum of Modern Art (MoMA) in New York City offers online classes on modern and contemporary art. These classes are designed to make art education available to students all over the world.
   Field Trips You Can Take Online
   Students and teachers are able to visit museums and other cultural institutions from any location in the world thanks to the advent of virtual field excursions. These virtual experiences typically feature live or pre-recorded tours, possibilities for direct engagement with museum educators, and interactive activities. The Smithsonian National Museum of Natural History offers students the opportunity to participate in virtual field trips, during which they can virtually explore the museum's exhibits and interact with museum experts.
5. **Digital Galleries and Museums That Can Be Visited Online**
   Museums that Utilize Virtual Reality
   Virtual reality museums provide visitors with an experience that is as close to being physically present as possible, allowing them to tour virtual galleries, view artworks, and interact with exhibits in the same way as if they were there in person. These online museums broaden the scope of cultural institutions and make the holdings of those organizations available to audiences all over the world. For instance, the Virtual Reality Museum of Fine Art provides users with a digital environment in which they can investigate well-known artworks and exhibitions.
   Online Showcases and Exhibits
   The physical collections of museums are often reimagined as virtual displays that are hosted on the museums' own websites. These displays may feature high-resolution photographs, full descriptions, and interactive elements, allowing visitors to interact with artworks and artifacts from their own devices, so

enhancing the visitor experience. The National Gallery of Art in Washington, District of Columbia, has a number of online exhibitions that provide access to the museum's collection in a digital format.

Platforms for Digital Artwork

The field of art has recently witnessed the proliferation of digital art platforms, which make it easier for artists to create, display, and sell their digital and virtual works of art. These platforms serve as a connection between the realm of technology and the art world, so opening up new doors of opportunity for both artists and collectors. There has been a rise in popularity of NFT (Non-Fungible Token) art platforms in the digital art arena. Some examples of these platforms include Rarible and SuperRare.

6. **Preservation and Remediation of Damage**

   Imaging with Digital Means for Historical Preservation

   The preservation and restoration of historical objects and works of art make use of many imaging methods, including digital imaging. Imaging techniques such as high-resolution imaging, infrared photography, and multispectral imaging unearth previously unseen features, underlying drawings, and structural problems. Conservators are able to make more educated decisions about the processes of restoration with the help of these technologies.

   Printing in 3D and scanning in 3D

   Technologies such as 3D printing and scanning are utilized in the process of replicating and restoring broken artifacts. Conservators can re-create lost or damaged components of sculptures, ceramics, or other items with an extraordinary level of precision using the techniques at their disposal. The reproduction of ancient objects for the purposes of research and education has been accomplished through the use of 3D printing in museums such as the British Museum.

   Observations of the Climate and the Environment

   Monitoring systems for the climate and environment are utilized by museums to ensure that the objects they house are kept in the best possible circumstances. These systems monitor factors like as temperature, humidity, light levels, and pollutants to ensure that things are kept and presented in the environment that is most suited to their needs. The Getty Conservation Institute has earned a well-deserved reputation for the important work it does in the field of environmental monitoring and preservation.

7. **Analysis of the Data and Interpretation of the Results**

   Analytics of Site Traffic

   In order to acquire insight into the ways in which people interact with exhibits and spaces, museums collect data on the behavior and preferences of museum visitors. Analytics of visitors provide useful information that can be used to inform the design of an exhibit, the flow of visitors, and interactive aspects. It is possible for museums to make use of data in order to improve the experience of visitors and boost engagement.

Customization of Website Content

Technology that enables personalization makes it possible for museums to cater the content they present to the preferences of individual visitors. Museums are able to deliver individualized recommendations to their guests by utilizing algorithms and collecting data from visitors. These may include suggested exhibits, tours, or further information. The visitor will feel a greater feeling of engagement and relevancy as a result of the use of personalization.

The combination of Artificial Intelligence (AI) and Machine Learning

The automation of the categorization and description of artifacts is made possible with the use of AI and machine learning algorithms. This makes it much simpler to manage collections and conduct research on them. These technologies also help curators with their work by identifying patterns and relationships among the museum's assets, which is one of their responsibilities.

8. **Difficulties and Things to Think About**

Accessibility in Digital Form It is of the utmost importance to make certain that all visitors, including those with impairments, have access to any and all technologically-driven advances. It is imperative that museums address concerns regarding accessibility and the usage of assistive technology.

Data Privacy: Since museums receive, record, and keep data about its visitors, there are legitimate concerns regarding the data's privacy and safety. In order to prevent unauthorized access to the personal information of visitors, organizations need to formulate transparent privacy policies and security measures.

Implementing new technology and continuing to upkeep existing systems both have associated costs. It is imperative that museums give careful consideration to the long-term financial commitments and viability of the technology-driven initiatives they undertake.

Finding a Happy Medium Between Tradition and Innovation Museums are challenged to strike a happy medium between upholding their long-held customs and embracing new forms of artistic and intellectual expression. It is essential to make certain that the use of technology improves, rather than detracts from, the experience of visitors.

The digital gap indicates that not all communities have equal access to the resources that are available online, despite the fact that technology has the potential to extend the reach of museums. It is imperative that museums address concerns of fairness in order to guarantee that everyone will benefit from technology.

A new epoch for cultural institutions has begun as a direct result of technological improvements made in museums. These advances have completely altered the experiences of visitors, increased the number of people who may access collections, and made the preservation efforts more effective. Technology is transforming the way in which museums carry out their goals, and this can be seen in everything from augmented reality and interactive exhibits to digital preservation and virtual museums. However, in order to continue utilizing technology for the betterment of local as well as global populations, museums will need to find solutions to issues concerning accessibility, data privacy, financial burdens, and equity. The incorporation of technology is not a break with history but rather a development that improves museums' capacity to engage, educate, and excite people in this era of digitalization.

7.1 Virtual reality and augmented reality in museums

The use of virtual reality (VR) and augmented reality (AR) technologies in museums has fundamentally altered the ways in which these cultural institutions interact with visitors and display their holdings. Visitors are able to explore historical environments, step inside artworks, and obtain a deeper knowledge of cultural items thanks to the immersive and interactive experiences offered by virtual reality (VR) and augmented reality (AR). These technologies bridge the gap between the physical world and the digital world, thereby enhancing the experiences of museum visitors and increasing the museums' overall reach. In the following paragraphs, we will discuss the impact that virtual reality and augmented reality have had on museums, as well as their applications, benefits, and challenges, and how they are playing a role in creating the future of cultural institutions.

1. **Utilization of Virtual Reality (VR) Equipment in Museums**
   Experience-Based Exhibitions
   The advent of virtual reality has made it possible for museums to construct immersive exhibitions that may take visitors to different eras and locations. Visitors can step into historical surroundings, such as ancient civilizations or key events, and experience them as if they were there by donning virtual reality headsets and entering those situations. The virtual reality experience is extremely immersive, allowing visitors to roam freely among the settings, interact with the various artifacts on display, and acquire a more in-depth knowledge of both history and culture.
   For instance, the "Time Machine" project at the British Museum makes use of virtual reality (VR) technology to recreate ancient settings and artifacts. This gives visitors the opportunity to investigate and engage with historical relics in a digital setting.
   Visualizations of Art in Galleries
   Virtual reality (VR) has been embraced by art institutions so that they can provide simulations of art galleries and exhibitions. Visitors are able to traverse virtually constructed galleries, view digital reproductions of the artworks, and access information in depth regarding each individual item. Virtual reality (VR) art gallery simulations provide visitors a novel approach to engage with and enjoy art by enabling them to go at their own pace while exploring the virtual

area and interacting with the items on display.

The Museum of Modern Art (MoMA) in New York City, for example, provides viewers with a genuine gallery experience by means of a virtual tour that enables them to explore the museum's collection without having to leave the comfort of their own homes.

Reconstructions based on archaeological and historical evidence

Virtual reality (VR) has shown to be a very helpful tool in the process of reconstructing archeological sites and historical environments. The use of virtual reality (VR) technology enables museums to reproduce historical events, architectural marvels, and ancient towns. These reconstructions allow guests to walk through them and receive insights into the past, which assists them in visualizing and comprehending the historical circumstances.

Virtual reality (VR) is used to create interactive experiences at the National Museum of Natural History in Washington, DC. These experiences allow visitors to explore ancient ecosystems and interact with extinct species.

Environments of Instruction That Are Interactive

Virtual reality (VR) is being implemented into educational settings to facilitate the development of interactive learning environments. Virtual reality (VR) allows museums to give students more immersive experiences while teaching them about art, history, and science. The educational experience can be made more engaging with the help of these settings by way of the incorporation of 3D models, virtual labs, and interactive simulations.

Students are given the opportunity to learn about art history while immersed in a virtual environment through the educational virtual reality (VR) experiences provided by the Getty Center in Los Angeles.

2. **Augmented reality (AR) in public spaces like museums**

Enhanced User Participation in Exhibits

The interactive capabilities of museum exhibitions are significantly improved by augmented reality. AR applications, which are generally accessed through mobile devices like smartphones and tablets, superimpose digital content over real-world objects. Using AR, guests will be able to access supplementary data, animations, or 3D models that are associated with the objects they are currently examining. The incorporation of this technology into the physical exhibits results in an increased level of interaction and context.

An augmented reality software is used at the Cleveland Museum of Art to provide visitors with interactive features. These aspects include information about artworks and the historical relevance of the artworks. The app provides a more customized experience by reacting to the visitor's location within the museum itself.

Contextualization of the Past and the Arts

Augmented reality applications at museums give visitors with additional historical and artistic context for the objects on display. Visitors can access multimedia content, such as audio guides, movies, and in-depth descriptions of artworks and objects, using their mobile devices. This content includes audio guides. Augmented reality (AR) brings the past and works of art to life by superimposing digital information that bolsters the visitor's comprehension of and enjoyment for the displays.

The Rijksmuseum in Amsterdam has developed an augmented reality software that offers visitors extensive information about the museum's collection. With this app, tourists are able to acquire a more in-depth comprehension of the artworks as well as the historical relevance of the objects.

Interactive Search and Rescue Missions

Inside of museums, augmented reality is frequently used to create interactive scavenger hunts and treasure hunts. These activities are designed to engage younger audiences as well as families, making trips to the museum not only entertaining but also informative. As part of the scavenger hunt experience, visitors use AR apps to go through puzzles, locate objects that have been concealed, and investigate a variety of displays.

An augmented reality (AR) scavenger hunt is available for families at the Smithsonian American Art Museum. This encourages kids to explore the museum's American art collection through an experience that is both interactive and game-like.

Communication and Physical Accessibility

AR applications are frequently used at museums as a means of overcoming language barriers and enhancing accessibility for a variety of audiences. Through the use of AR, guests can access information about the exhibit in a variety of languages, making it simpler for visitors from other countries and people who are not native speakers to comprehend the material.

For example, the Louvre Museum in Paris provides its visitors with an augmented reality app that presents information in a number of languages, guaranteeing that each individual can access content in the language that is most comfortable for them.

3. **The Value of Virtual Reality and Augmented Reality in Museums**
   Enhancement of Participation

   Virtual reality (VR) and augmented reality (AR) technologies enable experiences that are immersive and engaging, which both catch the attention of visitors and keep them interested. Through the use of these technologies, passive viewing can be transformed into active investigation, which enhances the experience as a whole.

   Possibilities for Furthering One's Education

   Virtual reality (VR) and augmented reality (AR) provide museums powerful educational tools.

They give historical context, interactive simulations, and in-depth information about artifacts and artworks, all of which contribute to the facilitation of learning. Because they cater to a wide variety of learning styles and age groups, these technologies make museums more accessible to students and people who continue to study throughout their lives.

Obtainability of Access

Virtual reality (VR) and augmented reality (AR) technology improve accessibility for guests with a variety of requirements. AR applications provide visitors with more information as well as language alternatives, whilst virtual reality (VR) enables visitors to explore exhibits in a virtual area, removing any physical limitations that may be present.

Personalized treatment

AR and VR make it possible to create uniquely individualized experiences. Museum goers have the ability to select which content they want to access, go around the displays at their own leisure, and personalize their experiences based on their unique interests. Through the use of personalization technology, museums are better able to accommodate a diverse variety of preferences.

Global Influence

Virtual reality (VR) and augmented reality (AR) are digital technologies, therefore museums can use them to reach people all over the world. Virtual experiences can be shared on the internet, which enables anyone from all over the world to remotely explore the collections of museums, whether for the sake of study, education, or leisure.

The practice of Conservation and Preserving

Virtual reality (VR) and augmented reality (AR) technology can be of assistance in the process of preserving objects and artworks.

Without having to physically handle fragile or broken artifacts, it is possible to examine and repair them using digital reproductions and 3D models that can be made.

4. **Obstacles and Important Considerations**

   The price as well as the availability

   The incorporation of virtual reality and augmented reality technology can be expensive, so it is important for museums to evaluate their budgets and the sources of their support. In addition, ensuring that visitors have access to the appropriate gear and software might be a difficulty. Not all visitors may have their own virtual reality headsets or smartphones with augmented reality capabilities, therefore it is possible that not all visitors will have access to the essential hardware and software.

   Construction of Contents

   The development of high-quality content for virtual reality and augmented reality applications demands a large investment of resources, including the expertise of designers, developers, and curators. To ensure that the technology improves the experience that visitors have at the museum, museums need to make investments in the creation of content.

Concerns about the Technology

The virtual reality (VR) and augmented reality (AR) technologies may have a variety of technical difficulties, including software bugs, device malfunctions, or connectivity challenges. In order to respond effectively and quickly to these difficulties, museums need to have support systems in place.

Privacy and protection of sensitive data

When employing virtual reality and augmented reality technologies, museums have a responsibility to address the implications for data privacy and security. When using these technologies to collect data on site visitors, you need to have clear policies and procedures in place to protect user information.

Striking a Balance Between Innovation and Tradition

It is imperative that museums strike a balance between upholding their long-standing customs and welcoming new forms of artistic and scientific expression. It is essential to make certain that the use of technology improves, rather than detracts from, the experience of visitors.

5. **The Future of Virtual Reality and Augmented Reality in Museums**

Enhanced Immersion: Virtual reality (VR) experiences may become even more immersive and realistic, enabling users to interact with places that are historically significant or artistically significant in ways that have never been possible before.

Integration of Artificial Intelligence Museums may choose to implement artificial intelligence in order to further tailor the experiences of their visitors. Virtual guides powered by AI could provide individualized recommendations as well as insights.

Collaborative and Multiplayer Experiences Virtual reality (VR) and augmented reality (AR) have the potential to provide collaborative experiences, in which visitors to an exhibit can explore it together, even if they are not in the same physical location. Virtual museum visits with multiple participants could encourage linkages and collaborative education.

Accessibility Improvements: Potentially, in the future, there will be an emphasis on accessibility improvements, with the goal of providing those with impairments or a variety of linguistic preferences with the opportunity to participate in virtual experiences.

Data-Driven Insights Virtual reality (VR) and augmented reality (AR) technology may be used by museums to collect and analyze visitor behavior data in order to improve exhibitions and increase engagement.

The museum experience has been completely transformed by the introduction of virtual reality and augmented reality, which provide opportunities for participation, teaching, and exploration that are immersive and interactive. Through the provision of historical context, interactive exhibitions, and chances for tailored learning, these technologies have contributed to an improvement in the tourist experience. However, in order to continue integrating virtual reality and augmented reality into their spaces, museums will need to overcome obstacles relating to cost, accessibility, content development, technological limitations, and privacy concerns. The usage of virtual reality (VR) and augmented reality (AR) is projected to grow in museums as technology continues to improve, which will increase the cultural institutions' accessibility as well as their teaching potential. These technologies bridge the gap between the physical world and the digital world, thereby altering the future of museums as well as the way in which we interact with art and cultural heritage.

7.2 Interactive exhibits and digital storytelling

Since the beginning of time, museums have fulfilled the role of treasuries for art, history, and cultural artifacts. They have, however, seen a substantial transition in recent years as a response to changing tourist expectations and developments in technology advancement. The museum experience has been fundamentally reimagined thanks in large part to the proliferation of interactive displays and digital narratives. The way in which museums interact with their audiences, construct immersive narratives, and bring the past to life has been fundamentally reimagined as a result of the development of novel technologies and methods. In the following paragraphs, we will discuss the impact that interactive exhibitions and digital storytelling have had on museums, as well as their applications, benefits, and challenges, as well as their role in determining the future of cultural institutions.

1. **The Participation of the Guest in Interactive Exhibits**
The Development of Museum Displays and Exhibits
The majority of conventional museum exhibitions take the form of stationary displays of relics or
pieces of art accompanied by explanatory labels. Although they are a good source of knowledge, most of the time they force visitors to take a back seat and simply observe. On the other side, interactive exhibitions encourage visitors to take an active role in interacting with the content on display, which results in a greater level of comprehension and appreciation for the topic at hand.
Learning by Doing or by Hand
Visitors are able to explore, experiment, and take an active role in the displays that are interactive. This type of learning is known as "hands-on learning." For instance, science museums frequently offer hands-on exhibits that allow visitors to engage in hands-on activities such as doing experiments, manipulating physical models, or participating in simulations in order to gain a better understanding of scientific principles.
The Mixed Realities of Augmented and Virtual Reality
The experience of visiting a museum has been fundamentally altered as a result

of the incorporation of augmented reality (AR) and virtual reality (VR) in interactive displays. These technologies provide experiences that are not just immersive and interactive but also often individualized. Visitors can gain a greater understanding of the material by using augmented reality (AR) and virtual reality (VR) to investigate historical surroundings, step inside artworks, or mimic archeological investigations.

Installations of interactive artworks

Art museums have increasingly begun to incorporate interactive exhibits, which give visitors the opportunity to interact with the artworks on display in fresh and exciting ways. Touch-sensitive screens, motion sensors, and sound-activated displays are examples of interactive art installation components that may be used. Visitors are encouraged to generate their own interpretations, play with the visual aspects, and even participate in the creation of the artwork.

For example, Random International's "Rain Room" installation creates an immersive and interactive art experience by allowing visitors to walk through a simulated rainfall. Sensors in the artwork ensure that the rain stops falling wherever a visitor is present, making the experience both real and relevant.

2. **The Art of Bringing Narratives to Life Through Digital Storytelling**

The Influence That Good Stories Can Have

Since the beginning of time, telling stories has been an essential component of human communication. It's a strong tool for engaging visitors, bringing the past to life, and communicating complicated information in a way that's appealing and easy to understand when applied to the context of museums. The use of technology to tell a tale in a more engaging manner is referred to as "digital storytelling."

Structure of a Narrative

Storytelling in the digital age frequently makes use of a structured narrative, in which information is presented in the form of a story that has a distinct beginning, middle, and conclusion. The narrative is typically presented to visitors of museums using a variety of digital mediums, including websites, mobile applications, and multimedia displays.

Components of Multimedia

Digital storytelling incorporates a variety of multimedia components, such as text, photos, audio, video, and interactive components, to produce an experience that is both more immersive and more compelling for the audience. Museums are able to more effectively transmit historical events, cultural traditions, and artistic trends with the assistance of these factors.

Personalized treatment

The telling of stories through digital media can be adapted to the specific tastes and passions of each individual.

Visitors are given the ability to choose their own courses through the various narratives, gain access to more material, and explore more deeply into particular areas of the story. The level of interaction and relevancy generated by visitors is increased via personalization.

3. **The Advantages of Utilizing Digital Storytelling and Interactive Exhibits**

   Participation from Visitors

   Exhibits that allow people to participate and digital narratives are two excellent ways to keep visitors interested. They turn visits to museums into dynamic and immersive experiences, captivating the interest of guests and encouraging them to actively participate in the activities.

   Having Educational Importance

   These tools have a significant instructional benefit since they simplify difficult concepts and make them easier to acquire and comprehend. Through hands-on experiences and information driven by narratives, visitors, and especially students and people who continue their education throughout their lives, can get a deeper grasp of history, science, art, and culture.

   Obtainability of Access

   The accessibility of varied audiences is improved through the use of interactive exhibitions and digital storytelling. It is possible for museums to provide supplementary content in a variety of languages, to make accommodations for people with impairments, and to make exhibits accessible to tourists from other countries.

   Personalized treatment

   Personalization is possible through the use of interactive exhibits as well as digital storytelling. A sense of ownership over one's visit to a museum can be gained when guests are given the opportunity to personalize their experiences to reflect their unique interests, preferences, and learning methods.

   Protecting Digital Content

   The preservation of cultural heritage and historical narratives can be greatly aided by the use of digital storytelling. It is possible for museums to make digital records of exhibitions, oral histories, and objects, making it possible for future generations to have access to these stories.

   Insights from the Data

   The utilization of interactive displays and digital storytelling in museums allows for the collection of significant data insights. Museums are able to keep track of the preferences and interactions of museum visitors, which enables the museums to improve its displays, content, and engagement tactics.

4. **Obstacles and Important Considerations**

   Expense and Available Resources

   The creation, installation, and ongoing upkeep of interactive exhibitions as well as digital storytelling can rack up significant costs. In order to ensure the success of these efforts, museums need to carefully analyze their financial limitations and distribute their resources in an efficient manner.

Construction of Contents

The production of high-quality content for interactive exhibitions and digital storytelling involves the involvement of a variety of specialized people. These professionals include curators, educators, multimedia specialists, and software developers. To provide visitors with experiences that are both entertaining and educational, museums need to make investments in the creation of new content.

Concerns about the Technology

It is possible for museums to experience a variety of technical difficulties, including hiccups in the program, problems with the hardware, or network concerns. It is absolutely essential to have support mechanisms in place in order to face these obstacles.

Privacy and protection of sensitive data

When adopting interactive technology, museums have a responsibility to address the implications for data privacy and security. When using these technologies to collect data on site visitors, you need to have clear policies and procedures in place to protect user information.

Striking a Balance Between Innovation and Tradition

It is imperative that museums strike a balance between upholding their long-standing customs and welcoming new forms of artistic and scientific expression. It is crucial to make certain that the use of technology improves, rather than detracts from, the experience of visitors.

5. **The Future of Museums, Including the Role of Digital Storytelling and Interactive Exhibits**

Enhanced Immersion: It is anticipated that technology will continue to improve immersion, making it possible for visitors to interact with displays in ways that are even more realistic and engaging.

Personalized AI Guides: Guides that are powered by artificial intelligence may become more advanced in the future, and they may provide visitors with personalized recommendations, insights, and interactive experiences that are catered to their particular areas of interest.

Participation in Collaborative Experiences Museums may investigate the possibility of participating in collaborative and multiplayer experiences. In these settings, visitors can study exhibits with one another, so establishing connections and shared learning.

Accessibility and Inclusivity: Future innovations will focus on increasing accessibility features, making interactive displays and digital storytelling available to individuals with disabilities, varying language preferences, and a variety of learning needs, and expanding opportunities for people to participate in these activities.

Integration of Augmented and Virtual Reality The incorporation of augmented and virtual reality into interactive exhibits and digital storytelling will result in the creation of additional options for immersive and engaging experiences.

Data-Driven Exhibits Museums will continue to make use of data insights in order to improve exhibits and increase the amount of interaction between visitors and the museum. When it comes to the optimization of content and interactive features, analytics will play a more prominent role.

The traditional museum experience has been revolutionized through the use of digital storytelling and interactive exhibits, which provide educational and exploratory opportunities for guests that are both immersive and engaging. These cutting-edge tools and methods create a bridge between the digital and physical worlds, thereby influencing the direction that cultural organizations will take in the future. As museums continue to harness technology to improve visitor engagement, accessibility, and education, they must confront obstacles relating to cost, the development of content, technical issues, the protection of privacy, and the preservation of traditions. It is expected that the role of interactive displays and digital storytelling in museums will continue to develop, which will enrich the experience of museum visitors and ensure the continuous relevance of these cultural institutions in a world that is rapidly transforming.

7.3 Online collections and virtual tours

The purpose of museums and other cultural organizations has always been to provide visitors with actual locations in which they can investigate art, history, and culture firsthand. The advent of the digital age, on the other hand, has ushered in a new era for these establishments by broadening their audience base and making them more accessible through the use of online collections and virtual tours. People from all over the world are able to access and engage with museum material thanks to these new ways, which has the effect of making cultural heritage more accessible than it has ever been. In this essay, we will investigate the effect that virtual tours and online collections have had on museums, as well as their uses, benefits, and challenges, as well as their role in determining the future of cultural institutions.

1. **The Merging of the Digital and Physical Worlds Through Online Collections**

   The Transformation Into the World Of Digital

   By digitizing their collections, museums have been making the slow but steady move into the digital world. In order to accurately portray artifacts, artworks, historical records, and other types of museum holdings in a digital format, this procedure requires the creation of high-resolution photos, 3D models, and multimedia information. Cultural heritage may now be viewed by people all over the world thanks to online collections, which also provide a wealth of information and new perspectives on the objects that are cared for by museums.

   Accessibility and dissemination of information

Museums are able to reach new audiences with their online collections, including those who
might not otherwise have the opportunity to visit the institution in person. The ability to access and explore cultural heritage from the comfort of one's own device is now available to international tourists, those with mobility issues, and people living in distant or neglected locations. Because of this increased accessibility, cultural interchange is encouraged, as is a deeper awareness of art, history, and culture.

Academic Study and Investigation

The availability of primary source materials and historical records made available through digital collections is beneficial to academic research and writing. Online access to these resources makes it possible for students, researchers, and academics to pursue academic endeavors more easily and contributes to a more profound comprehension of history and culture.

For example, the Library of Congress has an extensive digital collection that includes books, manuscripts, photos, and other historical resources. This makes the Library of Congress a great resource for researchers all around the world.

The Safekeeping of Our Cultural Traditions

The cultural heritage that is being preserved is helped by the digitization initiatives that are being made. The creation of digital copies of artifacts and documents to use as backups in the event that the originals become corrupted or lost helps to ensure that these items will be preserved for future generations. In addition, digital records eliminate the need for physical handling, which makes it possible to conduct in-depth studies and investigations of artifacts.

2. **Virtual Tours: Visiting Museums Without Leaving Your Home**
   Developing Content for Fully Immersive Experiences

   The museum experience may now be enjoyed in the comfort of the visitors' own homes thanks to virtual tours, which provide visitors immersive and interactive methods to explore the museum's halls and exhibits. These tours generally make use of 360-degree panoramic photos or video to give visitors the impression that they are actually present within the museum. Visitors are able to virtually move through the galleries, view artworks, and obtain information about the exhibits and objects on display.

   Possibilities for Furthering One's Education

   Significant educational opportunities can be found within of virtual tours. They are especially useful for schools and teachers since they offer students the opportunity to go on virtual field trips, during which they can experience museums and other cultural institutions from any location in the world. The guides for these tours may be live or pre-recorded, there may be possibilities for direct engagement with museum educators, and the tours may also involve interactive activities.

The Interaction of Cultures and Tourism

The ability for individuals to virtually visit museums all around the world contributes to the promotion of cultural exchange as well as tourism. Virtual tours allow visitors to preview museum spaces and exhibits before actually going there, which assists tourists in organizing their trips and enables them to make more educated decisions regarding their itineraries. These excursions also encourage a feeling of connection with the various sites and cultures that are visited.

Provision of Access for a Wide Range of Audiences

Accessibility for a wider range of audiences, including people with impairments, is improved by the use of virtual tours. These tours can be modified to meet the requirements of guests who have mobility issues, visual impairments, or other types of disabilities. Audio descriptions, alternative text, and keyboard navigation are all examples of features that contribute to inclusiveness.

3. The Advantages That Can Be Obtained From Utilizing Online Collections and Virtual Tours

Accessibility on a Global Scale

Through the use of online collections and virtual tours, cultural heritage can now be accessed all over the world. This has the effect of democratizing access to museums by allowing people from different regions of the world to study art, history, and culture without their having to travel.

Having Educational Importance

These online resources have a significant impact on educational outcomes. Students, teachers, and people who are learning throughout their lives have access to a variety of material and can participate in immersive learning experiences, which can result in a more profound comprehension of art, history, and culture.

Academic Study and Investigation

Access to primary source materials, historical documents, and artworks is made possible through the use of online collections, which in turn support study and scholarship. Even without direct access to the museum's holdings, researchers are able to undertake in-depth studies and come to novel conclusions about the museum's collections.

The Safekeeping of Our Cultural Traditions

Digital collections contribute to the preservation of cultural heritage by supplying digital backups and lowering the requirement for direct physical interaction with items. This helps ensure that museum holdings will be around for future generations to enjoy.

Ability to Participate and Accessibility

Accessibility and inclusivity are improved for a wide range of audiences because to the proliferation of online collections and virtual tours. These audiences include people with impairments, residents of rural areas, and tourists from other countries.

Tourism and Intercultural Communication

Individuals are given the opportunity to visit museums and other cultural institutions from the comfort of their own homes through the use of virtual tours, which in turn encourages tourism and the sharing of different cultures. They are a helpful resource for vacationers who are organizing their trips to the area.

4. **Obstacles and Important Considerations**

   Expense and Available Resources

   The production of online collections and the upkeep of virtual tours can require a significant investment of resources. The digitalization of museum collections, digital infrastructure, and the creation of new material all require budgetary support from museums.

   Superiority of the Content

   The success of online collections and virtual tours is directly proportional to how well the content is maintained at a high level of quality. Museums are responsible for ensuring that digital representations of artifacts and displays accurately reflect all of the nuances and intricacies of the objects being displayed.

   Problems of a Technical Nature

   There is a possibility that production and delivery of virtual tours will be plagued by technical difficulties. These issues include being compatible with a wide variety of devices and platforms, ensuring that navigation is smooth, and reducing load times as much as possible.

   Obtainability of Access

   For the purpose of making online collections and virtual tours available to people with disabilities, it is necessary to give careful thought to accessibility standards and guidelines. These standards and guidelines require, among other things, the provision of alternate formats, audio descriptions, and keyboard navigation.

   Privacy and Safety of Personal Information

   When collecting data about visitors through online platforms, museums are required to address concerns around data security and privacy. It is absolutely necessary to have transparent privacy rules and safety measures in place in order to protect user information.

5. **The Implications of Online Museum Collections and Virtual Tours for the Future of Museums**

Enhanced Immersion: In the future, virtual tours may become even more engaging and lifelike by utilizing cutting-edge technology such as augmented reality (AR) and virtual reality (VR) to provide tourists with experiences that are similar to those they would have in real life.

Accessibility in Multiple Languages: It is very possible that museums will increase their efforts to provide content in a variety of languages in order to appeal to audiences from all over the world. The use of machine translation and tour guides fluent in multiple languages might become more prevalent.

Interactive Educational Tools Virtual tours will continue to develop as educational tools, eventually providing students and tourists with an increased number of interactive activities, quizzes, and educational resources to keep their interest.

Inventions in Accessible Technologies: Future advancements will center on improving accessibility technologies to cater to various audiences, including individuals with disabilities, in order to provide a digital museum experience that is more welcoming to people with a wider range of abilities.

Insights that are Driven by Data: Museums will employ data insights gained from online collections and virtual tours to improve user experiences, optimize content, and further develop accessible features.

Access to museums and cultural assets has been reimagined thanks to the proliferation of online collections and virtual tours, which have helped to close the gap between the analog and digital worlds. These creative ways make cultural heritage more accessible, engaging, and instructional, and the benefits of this accessibility and engagement and education extend to a wide variety of audiences and academics. However, museums must handle obstacles relating to cost, content quality, accessibility, and data privacy as they continue to employ technology to enhance visitor experiences. These challenges can be broken down into five categories: technical concerns, content issues, accessibility issues, and content quality issues. It is expected that the role of online collections and virtual tours in museums will grow, which will foster cultural interchange, increased accessibility on a worldwide scale, and a more profound appreciation of art, history, and culture in this day of rapid technological advancement.

7.4 Challenges and opportunities of technology in museums

The use of technology in museums poses a number of obstacles as well as opportunities that profoundly impact the manner in which cultural institutions operate and interact with the audiences they serve.

The Obstacles:

The implementation and upkeep of technology can be resource-intensive and expensive endeavors, necessitating significant financial commitments.

It is often difficult for museums to maintain adequate budgets, which makes it difficult for them to stay up with the most recent technical breakthroughs and improvements.

Accessibility and Inclusivity: Although technology has the potential to improve accessibility, it is still a struggle to make sure that it is accessible and inclusive for all visitors, including those who have disabilities. It is imperative that museums place an emphasis on accessibility features and address concerns regarding the digital divide and the availability of assistive devices.

Development of Content and Curation In order to develop and curate high-quality digital content, trained individuals are required. These skilled experts include curators, educators, and digital specialists. The goal of preserving content that is both captivating and educational can be one that requires a lot of resources for museums.

Concerns Regarding Data Security and Privacy are Raised When Visitor Data Is Collected and Managed using Technology The collection and management of visitor data using technology creates concerns regarding data security and privacy. In order to prevent information on museum visitors from being stolen or misused, museums need to formulate transparent data privacy rules and procedures.

Occasions to seize:

Increased Visitor Engagement Technology presents new potential for immersive and interactive experiences, which in turn increases the level of engagement that visitors have with museum material and fosters a stronger relationship with that content.

The ability to access a global audience through the use of online platforms, virtual tours, and digital collections gives museums the ability to extend their sphere of influence and impact beyond the confines of their physical locations.

The availability of cutting-edge educational technologies that are adaptable to a variety of students' preferred modes of instruction has resulted in an increase in the educational value of museum visits for students, teachers, and people who continue their education throughout their lives.

Insights Driven by Data: Museums can acquire significant insights into the preferences and behaviors of visitors by leveraging data analytics. This enables the museums to adjust their experiences, exhibits, and activities to match the specific requirements and interests of their audiences.

Preservation and Conservation: Technology plays an important role in the preservation and conservation of artifacts and artworks. This is because it makes it possible to conduct in-depth analyses, create digital replications, and engage in long-term conservation efforts in order to preserve cultural heritage for future generations.

It is possible for museums to continue to develop and grow as important cultural and educational organizations in the digital age by overcoming the problems brought by technology and making the most of the opportunities that technology offers.

Chapter 8

Museums in a Global Context

There is a great deal more to museums than just the storage of historical artifacts and relics. On a worldwide basis, they are dynamic institutions that play a crucial part in the process of maintaining culture, developing understanding, and shaping individual and collective identities. Over the course of several centuries, these institutions have developed by responding to shifts in the surrounding sociocultural, technological, and political landscapes. Within the context of the world as a whole, museumss have developed into strong venues for education, conversation, and the transmission of knowledge. We will dive into the historical development of museums, their function in the preservation of cultural heritage, their contribution to education and research, as well as their influence on the formation of identities and the promotion of international understanding as part of this all-encompassing investigation of museums in the context of the wider world.

The Development of Museums Throughout History

The concept of museums as stores of historical information and cultural artifacts extends back thousands of years. The practice of collecting and exhibiting relics, works of art, and other oddities may be traced back to ancient civilizations such as Egypt, Greece, and Rome. These civilizations were known to have museums. However, during the Renaissance in Europe, the modern idea of museums as institutions dedicated to the conservation and presentation of cultural and historical artifacts began to take shape.

During this time period, collecting artifacts from a variety of civilizations and putting them on display became a common pastime among the affluent people of Europe, particularly the Medici family who lived in Florence, Italy. The collection amassed by the Medici family, which came to be known as the "cabinet of curiosities," had a significant role in paving the way for the establishment of museums. This idea quickly extended to other countries in Europe, leading to the formation of private collections as well as institutions that were built specifically for the purpose of providing the general public with access to displays of works of art, antiques, and natural history specimens.

The founding of the Ashmolean Museum at the University of Oxford in 1683 is often regarded as one of the most pivotal moments in the development of museums as we know them today. It was the first public museum in England, and it was established with the intention of making its art and artifact collections freely accessible to the general public.

The Ashmolean Museum is credited with helping to establish a standard for other public museums to follow and for contributing to the notion that cultural assets should be open to the general public.

The world experienced a boom in the acquisition of artifacts from faraway regions throughout the 18th and 19th centuries as a direct result of the expansion of both colonialism and exploration. These items, which were collected by European explorers, were frequently put on display in cabinets of curiosities or served as the basis for the establishment of new natural history and ethnographic museums. These institutions were occasionally troublesome because they failed to understand the cultural significance of the things that they presented and instead treated them as ordinary curiosities. This resulted in the objects being seen as less than they actually were.

As the 19th century proceeded, there was a rising realization of the necessity to preserve cultural heritage and the role that museums played in doing so. This led to the establishment of many new museums throughout the world. This resulted in the founding of national museums as well as the development of professional standards for the management of museums, the curation of their collections, and the preservation of historical artifacts. Since its establishment in 1753, the British Museum has served as a prototype for the encyclopedic museum. It is home to a large collection of works of art and artifacts from all over the world.

Institutions in the United States, such as the Smithsonian Institution, which was established in 1846, played a comparable role in the conservation and display of cultural and scientific artifacts around the country. By encouraging a greater emphasis on research, education, and public access, these institutions played a critical role in molding the terrain of the modern museum landscape.

The Importance of Museums in Preserving Cultural Heritage Around the World

The protection of cultural heritage is widely recognized as one of the most important roles that museums play in the modern world. Museums provide as storage facilities for artifacts, works of art, and other objects that represent the history, values, and identities of a variety of different cultural groups. They play an essential part in preserving these assets for future generations, ensuring that they are safeguarded against degradation, theft, or destruction in any of those three ways.

Artifacts of Culture and Works of Art: Museums are known to house a wide variety of cultural artifacts, some of which include paintings, sculptures, textiles, and decorative arts. The artistic accomplishments of various cultures throughout history can be better understood because to the information provided by these objects.

For instance, the Louvre Museum in Paris holds a great collection of art, one of which is the world-famous Mona Lisa, which exemplifies the creative prowess of the Italian Renaissance.

Artifacts from Ancient Civilizations That Have Been Discovered There Are Numerous Museums That Focus Exclusively On Archaeological Artifacts, Which Help Us Understand the Routines And Customs Of Ancient Civilizations. For example, the Egyptian Museum in Cairo is home to a spectacular collection of antiquities from ancient Egypt. These items offer insight on the culture and beliefs of the pharaohs who ruled Egypt during that time.

Collections of Ethnographic Artifacts: The primary focus of ethnographic museums is on the material culture of indigenous peoples from all over the world. These collections teach us to understand the variety of human communities and the distinctive ways in which people choose to live their lives. The Pitt Rivers Museum in Oxford, for instance, is an example of an establishment that possesses a sizeable ethnographic collection and exhibits a diverse range of artifacts originating from a variety of different civilizations.

Specimens from the Field of Natural History Specimens of flora and wildlife can be found at natural history museums, which can provide information regarding the biodiversity of our planet. An excellent illustration of a museum that is committed to protecting the natural history of the planet is the American Museum of Natural History in New York City. This museum is known for its extensive collection of dinosaur fossils.

Intangible Heritage: Certain museums, such as those on the UNESCO Intangible Cultural Heritage Lists, are dedicated to the preservation of intangible cultural heritage, which includes customs, rites, music, and performing arts among other things. These institutions contribute to the preservation of the cultural legacy of a variety of communities.

In addition to preserving their collections, museums also participate in activities such as restoring and conserving them to ensure that their collections are kept in pristine shape. In order to restore and preserve antiquities and works of art, museums frequently work in conjunction with specialists such as conservators. These preservation measures are absolutely necessary if we are going to extend the lives of cultural assets and ensure that future generations will be able to study and learn from them.

The Roles of Education and Investigation in Museums

Museums are not merely archival storage facilities; rather, they have evolved into vibrant educational institutions that fulfill a wide variety of functions. They play an important part in both official and informal education by giving visitors the opportunity to learn about art, history, science, and culture in ways that are interesting and interactive. In addition, museums play an important role in the growth of knowledge across a variety of disciplines since they serve as centers for study.

Formal Education: There is a long tradition of museums working together with other educational institutions to improve student learning inside the classroom. It is common practice for educators to use museums as an extension of the classroom, giving students the opportunity to investigate real-world applications of history, science, and art. The provision of educational programs, workshops, and guided tours is typical of museums located all around the world.

Informal Education Museums have a significant role in both official and informal education. Participating in exhibits, interacting with hands-on displays, and attending lectures or workshops are all options open to visitors of any age. These experiences stimulate curiosity and lead to a more profound comprehension of the world, so making museums more approachable to a large number of people.

Research and scholarship are two of the pillars upon which museums are built. They frequently make use of specialists from a wide variety of subjects to carry out study on their holdings. For instance, museum curators, historians, archaeologists, and scientists all collaborate in an effort to deepen our comprehension of the items and specimens housed at these institutions. Their investigation frequently results in the unveiling of hitherto unknown facts, the formulation of previously unknown hypotheses, and the writing of scholarly articles.

Archiving and Cataloguing: In order to properly categorize and archive their collections, museums keep detailed catalogs and databases. Scholars and researchers can gain access to knowledge regarding items and objects that may not be on show to the general public by making use of these resources, which are of great value to these groups. Museums are an essential part of the process of passing on information to next generations.

Contribution to Science The act of keeping and analyzing specimens is a significant way in which natural history museums, in particular, contribute to scientific research. The documentation of biodiversity, the carrying out of taxonomic studies, and the contribution to a greater understanding of ecosystems and evolutionary biology are all common areas of collaboration between museums and scientists and researchers.

Museums play a crucial role as partners in the educational environment because they provide invaluable materials and experiences that not only improve learning but also build a greater appreciation for a wide range of topics. Students and members of the general public both benefit from these events since they foster the development of research skills, critical thinking, and cultural awareness.

Developing one's sense of self while also contributing to global comprehension

Museums have the ability to mold people's identities, both individually and collectively, on a local as well as a more global scale. They are influential in the way that they convey and interpret cultural and historical tales, offering a platform for communities to reflect on their past and the more general experience of being human. In addition, museums have the potential to contribute to a better understanding of international issues by encouraging interaction and empathy between people of other cultures and societies.

Frequently, museums are able to convey the identity of the local populations that they are tasked to serve. They offer a venue where the history and culture of the community can be honored and maintained over time. Communities are better able to connect with their ancestry and roots when they have access to local museums that highlight regional history, art, and customs.

National Museums Play a Significant part in Shaping a Country's Identity National museums play an important part in shaping the identity of a country by presenting its history, achievements, and cultural assets. For instance, the National Museum of China in Beijing showcases the extensive history and culture of China, which contributes to a stronger sense of both national pride and identity.

Perspective on the World Many museums work toward the goal of fostering a perspective on the world as a whole by exhibiting the interconnection of human history and culture. They frequently put on exhibits that investigate interactions between people of different cultures, globalization, and experiences that people have in common. For example, the collection of items from all over the world that can be found in the British Museum highlights the interconnected character of human history.

Museums have the potential to act as diplomatic tools, making possible cultural interaction and collaboration between nations as part of cultural diplomacy. Exhibitions and partnerships held on a global scale help advance diplomatic relations and cross-cultural understanding. One such cultural cooperation that encourages two-way communication between France and the United Arab Emirates is represented by the Louvre Abu Dhabi, which is a satellite location of the Louvre Museum in Paris.

Museums provide sites for discourse and debate on major social and political topics, and they play a vital role in the promotion of dialogue. The majority of the time, they are the ones in charge of curating exhibitions that tackle modern issues such as migration, social justice, and climate change. These displays have the potential to stimulate introspective and empathetic thought, in addition to open and candid communication.

The presentation of alternate viewpoints and voices can be one way for museums to challenge the dominant narratives and assumptions that are held in their communities. They have the ability to rewrite historical accounts and put light on stories that have been neglected or suppressed in the past. The National Museum of African American History and Culture in Washington, District of Columbia, examines the history of African Americans while posing questions to the conventional stories that have been told about their past.

Museums have a significant role to play in the formation of both individual and communal identities. People are able to better understand the larger context of human history, celebrate their past, and connect with where they came from thanks to these resources. At the same time, they provide possibilities for engagement across cultural boundaries, which helps to foster tolerance, empathy, and a common sense of humanity.

In a Global Context, We Face Both Obstacles and Opportunities

In a global environment, museums present a number of opportunities and challenges, despite the fact that they have a tremendous amount of promise for the preservation of cultural heritage, education, and increased international understanding. It is imperative that these concerns be addressed in order to guarantee that museums will continue to thrive and perform the important functions for which they are responsible.

The Obstacles:

Accessibility: Museums have a responsibility to make certain that its collections may be viewed by everybody, regardless of their socioeconomic standing or physical disabilities. This includes making collections available online and building physical venues that are accessible to people with disabilities.

Repatriation and Restitution The question of whether or not cultural relics should be returned to their original homes is one that has sparked a contentious and ongoing discussion. A great number of museums are struggling with issues of ownership and restitution, particularly in relation to artifacts that were stolen during the time of colonialism.

Money and Sustainability: Museums frequently have trouble obtaining money and remaining sustainable, which can hinder their ability to build and preserve collections, run educational programs, and undertake research.

Diversity and Inclusion: Museums are required to address issues of diversity, equity, and inclusion in all aspects of their operations, including both their staffing and their programming. This entails presenting a wide variety of viewpoints and voices in the exhibitions as well as the interpretation of the content.

Transformation in the Digital Age While the digital age affords museums with potential to expand their reach, it also brings issues connected to digitization, copyright, and internet security.

Occasions to seize:

Engagement in the Virtual World The advent of the digital era has made it possible for museums to communicate with audiences all over the world through the use of virtual tours, online exhibitions, and interactive experiences. This broadens the scope of their influence and reach.

Engagement of the Community: Museums have the potential to become community hubs by inviting local residents to participate in the exhibition selection process and educational programming. This helps people feel like they own something and that they belong somewhere.

Collaboration Across Institutions: Museums have the ability to work with other types of institutions, such as libraries, archives, and universities, to combine their respective resources and bodies of information, thereby producing more exhaustive research and programming.

Practices That Contribute to a More Sustainable Future A growing number of museums are implementing practices that contribute to a more sustainable future. These practices include energy-efficient operations and ecologically friendly exhibitions.

In today's interconnected world, museums have evolved into dynamic institutions that play a variety of roles. They are not only responsible for the preservation of cultural heritage, but also serve as centers of teaching and research that contribute to our overall comprehension of the world. Additionally, museums have the ability to mold identities, which contributes to increased regional, national, and international comprehension.

As we progress farther into the 21st century, museums are presented with a variety of opportunities as well as obstacles. In the areas of digital transformation, community engagement, and sustainable practices, museums have the potential to continue their evolution and make an impact that will stay. In our increasingly linked world, if museums are able to manage these issues and capitalize on these opportunities, they will continue to be key contributors to the preservation of cultural traditions, the education of future generations, and the promotion of understanding.

The ability of museums to adapt, develop, and keep their dedication to preserving cultural heritage, spreading knowledge, and encouraging international understanding is essential to their continued success and relevance in a global setting. By doing so, museums will continue to contribute to the collective worldwide experience of humanity and enrich the lives of those who visit them.

8.1 International cooperation in the museum world

The role of preserving cultural heritage, storing historical items, and providing educational opportunities has been played by museums for a very long time. The importance that museums play in our increasingly globalized world extends beyond than their particular communities and the nations in which they are located. The rich fabric of human culture and history may be preserved, shared, and celebrated with a significant amount of help from international cooperation in the museum sector. This essay takes a deep dive into the numerous facets of international cooperation in the museum sector, analyzing how it promotes cultural exchange, protects legacy, and furthers global understanding.

1. **Making Possible Intercultural Communication**
   International cooperation in the museum sector serves as a catalyst for cultural exchange by making it possible to share artistic, historical, and scientific assets across international borders. This exchange works in both directions, allowing museums to work together on exhibitions, research projects, and educational programs that not only highlight the museums' own collections but also expose local audiences to the cultures of other parts of the world.

Joint Exhibitions: The organization of joint exhibitions is one of the most obvious types of international cooperation in museums today. It is common practice for museums located in other nations to work together in order to exhibit works of art, artifacts, or topics that transcend national boundaries. These exhibitions introduce local audiences to the cultural environment of other countries and build a broader awareness for the diversity that exists around the world.

For instance, the "Terracotta Warriors: Guardians of Immortality" exhibition was a joint effort between the Shaanxi History Museum in China and the National Gallery of Victoria in Australia. This exhibition brought the well-known Terracotta Army and other Chinese relics to the attention of audiences in Australia. This cultural exchange not only contributed to the enhancement of Australia's cultural landscape but also served to improve communication between the two countries.

Exchange Programs: Museums frequently participate in exchange programs, in which they lend their collections to other establishments and display artifacts from other countries in their own galleries. These programs promote understanding across different cultures and provide chances for museum workers to exchange their knowledge and expertise with one another.

For example, the Louvre Museum in Paris participates in a number of exchange programs with museums all around the world. These programs allow works of art and other items from the Louvre's collection to be displayed at partner museums and vice versa. This method to trade, which is based on mutual benefit and reciprocity, creates worldwide relationships and cultural diplomacy.

The practice of fostering international collaboration through the establishment of museums might be considered a sort of cultural diplomacy. The diplomatic ties between countries can be strengthened through the promotion of mutual understanding and the facilitation of conversation through collaborative projects. Museums can help contribute to constructive international relations by presenting the history, culture, and artifacts of a country with which they are partnered.

2. **The Conservation of Heritage Across National Boundaries**

The protection of cultural assets frequently occurs outside of the context of national boundaries. A great number of artifacts and pieces of art are significant from a historical or cultural perspective to more than one nation or community. In the world of museums, international cooperation is an absolutely necessary component in the process of preserving and safeguarding these invaluable pieces of our common history.

There may be historical artifacts on display at museums all around the world that are connected to one another in some way. It's possible that over the course of time, certain pieces of history became divided as a result of numerous historical events or colonial activities. With the support of international cooperation, these shards of information can be pieced back together to provide a more complete picture of our collective past.

The Rosetta Stone is a well-known illustration of this phenomenon; it was discovered in Egypt, yet it is now housed in the British Museum.

Through their joint efforts, the Egyptian government and the British Museum were able to reach a consensus over the significance of this important relic. These types of partnerships highlight the significance of international cooperation in the process of connecting historical accounts.

Cooperation Between Museums Is Essential For The Protection Of legacy In times of conflict, looting, or natural catastrophes, cooperation between museums is essential for the protection of legacy. It is possible for museums to play a part in the process of identifying items that have been stolen or illegally trafficked, campaigning for their recovery, and assuring their safekeeping during times of crisis.

While establishments such as the Louvre, the British Museum, and the Metropolitan Museum of Art in New York City work together to assist the preservation of cultural heritage in areas that are experiencing violence, organizations such as INTERPOL and UNESCO partner with museums to locate and recover objects that have been stolen.

3. **Increasing Comprehension Across the World**

It is possible for museums to contribute to a better understanding of the world as a whole by encouraging conversations between people of different cultures, exposing and debunking stereotypical beliefs, and fostering the free flow of ideas. Because it pushes museums to move beyond national narratives and fosters a more comprehensive and inclusive perspective of our common human history, international cooperation in the museum field is a strong instrument in this regard.

Museums frequently address the prejudices and misconceptions that people have about other cultures, locations, or peoples in order to challenge those notions. Museums may question and correct these beliefs by presenting images of the world that are more complex and realistic. This can be accomplished through international collaborations between museums.

For instance, the National Museum of African American History and Culture in Washington, District of Columbia, challenges historical clichés by putting the African American experience in a more general framework. The museum's mission is to preserve and present the African American experience. Through its exhibitions and educational programs, the Museum of Islamic Art in Doha, Qatar, attempts to challenge misconceptions and stimulate dialogue about Islamic culture and history. This mission is similar to that of the Museum of Islamic Art in Istanbul, Turkey.

Legacy That We All Share International cooperation in the museum sector brings attention to the common legacy that all people share. This highlights the fact that, on a fundamental level, the experiences, aspirations, and expressions of all cultures are interrelated with one another. This point of view fosters feelings of empathy and understanding among people from other cultures and countries.

The United Nations Educational, Scientific, and Cultural Organization (UNESCO) runs a program called World Heritage, which recognizes places of cultural, historical, or ecological significance as being worthy of preservation. These designations highlight the significance of our collective history as well as the necessity of international cooperation in order to ensure its preservation.

Museums have the potential to serve as platforms for dialogue on topics that are relevant in today's world. The results of international cooperation frequently take the form of exhibitions that investigate contemporary issues confronting the global community, such as climate change, migration, and human rights. Conversation, in-depth thought, and the sharing of perspectives are all fostered by these displays.

4. **Opportunities and Obstacles in the Field of International Museum Collaboration**

International cooperation in the museum sector has the potential to bring about a great many benefits; nevertheless, it also poses a number of problems that will need to be overcome in order for it to be both effective and sustainable.

The Obstacles:

When working together on exhibitions or projects, it is essential to be sensitive to the various cultures represented and the distinctions and sensitivities that accompany them. Controversies or strained relationships between nations and museums might be the result of misunderstandings or a lack of sensitivity toward particular subjects.

Questions of Ownership and Repatriation: When it comes to international museum cooperation, questions of ownership and repatriation continue to be among the most problematic challenges. Some countries have made it clear that they want the items and artworks that were taken from them during times of colonial rule or under questionable circumstances returned.

The movement of antiques and works of art can be complicated by a number of factors, including international law, ethical considerations, export and import rules, and domestic laws. In order to ensure that they are in compliance, museums need to negotiate these concerns carefully.

The amount of money that is typically spent on international collaboration can be considered to be a major expense. It is frequently difficult to obtain money for collaborative initiatives, such as those involving transportation, environmental protection, and insurance.

Occasions to seize:

Participation in the Digital Age: New possibilities for worldwide museum collaboration are presented by digital technology. Museums now have the ability to engage audiences all over the world and work on a much bigger scale thanks to virtual exhibitions, online collections, and collaborative digital platforms.

Involvement of Communities: International collaborations have the potential to involve local communities in both of the partner nations, which can develop a sense of ownership and a sense of shared responsibility for cultural heritage.

Education and Research: Institutions are able to share their knowledge and skills through the formation of joint educational programs and research projects that can result from collaborative efforts.

Sustainability: The promotion of sustainable practices can be made possible by international cooperation, such as coordinated conservation efforts, energy-efficient displays, and environmentally friendly methods of transportation.

In the field of museums, international cooperation is a multifaceted and powerful force that promotes cultural exchange, protects legacy, and furthers global understanding. The development of linkages between nations, the dismantling of stereotypical beliefs, and the promotion of a common global heritage are all significantly aided by museums. Through international museum cooperation, there are significant chances for cultural diplomacy, mutual enrichment, and education. Although there are obstacles to overcome, such as cultural sensitivity, ownership issues, and resource limits, there are also enormous opportunities.

The importance of museums as worldwide bridges of cultural understanding and preservation will continue to develop as our planet becomes increasingly interconnected. Museums have the capacity to transcend borders and promote a global community that is more inclusive and empathic, one in which the wealth of human culture and history is honored, shared, and safeguarded for the generations to come.

8.2 The role of museums in fostering cross-cultural understanding

Museums play an important role as crucial institutions for the purpose of preserving and presenting the varied cultural legacy of humanity. In addition to their roles as storage facilities for works of art, historical artifacts, and scientific data, museums play an important part in advancing international comprehension. They create opportunity for people to learn about, appreciate, and respect the traditions and histories of others by serving as platforms for education, conversation, and the cultivation of empathy. In this article, we will investigate the many facets of the role that museums play in fostering intercultural understanding. Specifically, we will investigate the ways in which museums encourage cultural interchange, combat stereotypical thinking, advance inclusivity, and contribute to world peace.

1. **Making Possible Intercultural Communication**
People are able to connect with the cultural assets of other groups through the medium of museums. They make cultural interchange possible by bringing the

world to the doorsteps of tourists and letting them to study different art forms, historical tales, and cultural traditions from throughout the world.

Exhibitions: One of the key ways museums develop understanding between other cultures is via the presentation of exhibitions that highlight the art, artifacts, and tales of a variety of different cultures. Visitors are able to enter other worlds through the exhibitions, whether they are interested in the ancient history of Egypt, the dynamic traditions of India, or the current art scene in Japan. It has been shown that international collaborative exhibitions, in which museums work together with institutions from different nations, are particularly beneficial in increasing intercultural understanding. For example, the "Silk Road: Treasures from Xinjiang" exhibition, which was a joint effort between the National Museum of China and the Louvre, was able to educate people all over the world about the prosperous history of the Silk Road. People are encouraged to develop an appreciation for the interconnection of human civilizations through the use of exhibitions such as these.

Participating in international collaborations and exchanges is an important aspect of cultural diplomacy, which is another way in which museums contribute to the field. These types of partnerships have the potential to bolster diplomatic connections, advance mutual comprehension, and make it easier for nations to communicate with one another. It is possible for museums to greatly contribute to the improvement of international relations through the exhibition of the culture and legacy of a country with which they are partnered.

For instance, the Abu Dhabi branch of the Guggenheim Museum in the United Arab Emirates aspires to be a center for cultural exchange. Its mission is to promote understanding between the East and the West by holding exhibitions and events that highlight traditional as well as contemporary art from a variety of countries.

2. **Subverting Assumptions and Preconceptions**

   Museums offer a one-of-a-kind opportunity to combat preconceived notions and generalizations on a variety of various cultures. They can provide visitors with depictions of the world that are more complex and realistic, which encourages visitors to go beyond generalizations and preconceived beliefs.

   The National Museum of African American History and Culture in Washington, District of Columbia, is an excellent illustration of a museum that combats stereotypical portrayals of its subject matter. It highlights the accomplishments, hardships, and resiliency of the African American community by presenting the African American experience within the larger framework of American history through its exhibitions and collections. By doing so, the museum challenges commonly held beliefs and provides visitors with an understanding of the history of
   African Americans that is both more thorough and more compassionate.

One other establishment, the Museum of Islamic Art in Doha, Qatar, is working to dispel negative preconceptions about Islamic culture and history by encouraging open discussion about these topics. It does this by hosting exhibitions, running programs, and engaging in outreach activities with the hopes of addressing common misunderstandings regarding Islam and the Middle East and promoting a deeper level of comprehension.

3. **Fostering an Attitude of Inclusivity**

By encouraging inclusivity, museums can make important contributions to bridging the gap between different cultures. They make possible the celebration and valuing of the many voices, opinions, and stories that come from a variety of cultural backgrounds by creating venues.

The concept of multiculturalism is celebrated in a lot of museums, and one way they do this is by recognizing the achievements that many cultural groups within one community have made. An excellent illustration of a museum that places an emphasis on both inclusivity and multiculturalism is the Canadian Museum for Human Rights, which can be found in Winnipeg, Canada. It examines topics pertaining to human rights from a variety of cultural and historical vantage points, with a focus on the significance of mutual understanding, tolerance, and cooperation across distinct cultures.

Community Engagement Museums actively engage with the communities that surround them and actively encourage community members to participate in museum exhibitions and other museum-sponsored activities. The members of the community are more likely to have a feeling of ownership and belonging as a result of this, which increases the likelihood that their cultural heritage and points of view will be acknowledged and honored.

4. **Initiating Conversations And Trying To Get People To Think Critically**

Museums are lively learning settings that foster conversation, debate, and critical thinking and are well worth visiting. Museums are able to provide opportunity for visitors to engage with diverse cultures and points of view by providing exhibits that are not only intricate but also thought-provoking.

Issues of the Present Day: It is common practice for museums to investigate issues of the present day, including climate change, migration, human rights, and social justice. These issues provoke visitors' critical reflection on the interdependence of the world and on the ramifications of adopting various points of view and courses of action.

Programs for Education: Museums typically provide a wide variety of educational programs, including seminars, lectures, and guided tours, all of which are designed to engage visitors in thought-provoking conversations. Individuals are able to gain a deeper understanding of a variety of cultures by participation in these programs, which offer a platform for learning and exchange.

5. **The Relationship to International Identities**

Individuals are better able to connect with their global identity thanks to the function that museums play in the process. They assist individuals in developing an appreciation for the interdependence of human history, culture, and society. Museums foster a sense of solidarity and empathy that is not limited by the confines of a particular nation, ethnic group, or religious tradition. This is accomplished by displaying the common heritage of all people.

UNESCO World Heritage Sites: The UNESCO World Heritage program acknowledges the significance of shared world heritage by designating certain locations as World Heritage Sites. By naming some locations of cultural, historical, or ecological significance as World Heritage Sites, the importance of international cooperation in the preservation of these areas is brought to light. These locations highlight the connectivity of many civilizations as well as the significance of conserving the history we all have in common.

In a world that is becoming more interconnected, museums are becoming increasingly important institutions for the promotion of intercultural understanding. They promote inclusivity, challenge prejudices and misconceptions, encourage conversation and critical thinking, bring the treasures of the globe to local audiences, and connect individuals to their global identities. In short, they make cultural interchange possible. Museums help to foster empathy, tolerance, and collaboration by bridging the gaps that can sometimes exist between communities and cultures that are very different from one another.

It is extremely important that museums continue to play a leading role in promoting intercultural understanding as we continue to negotiate the difficulties of our increasingly globalized environment. Museums have the ability to remove barriers, pique visitors' interests, and foster a profound appreciation for the wealth and variety of our worldwide human past. Museums contribute to a society that is more harmonious and interconnected through education, dialogue, and the celebration of cultural differences. This creates an environment in which cross-cultural understanding is not only feasible but also valued.

Chapter 9

The Future of Museums

Over the course of history, museums, which were previously thought of as unchanging receptacles for objects, have undergone tremendous transformations. They are confronted with new problems and opportunities that are reshaping the future of these cultural organizations as a result of the fast transforming world we live in today. The functions that museums play, the advances that technology makes, and the increased emphasis that is placed on being environmentally responsible are all characteristics of the future of museums. During this in-depth examination of the subject, we are going to dig into the ways in which museums are evolving their functions, the impact that technology is having, the role that inclusivity and diversity play, the relevance of sustainability, and the potential problems and opportunities that lie ahead.

1. **The Changing Functions of Museums**
1. **Centers for Educational and Community Engagement:**
    Museums are increasingly being recognized as hubs for learning and community participation. They make learning accessible to visitors by way of hands-on exhibitions, workshops, and lectures, as well as other educational programming. Museums are no longer considered to be passive environments; rather, they invite visitors to actively participate and think critically. Traditional academic disciplines are no longer the only ones covered in school; instead, education now encompasses a wider range of themes, including environmental sustainability, social justice, and cultural awareness.
2. **Places for Community and Social Interaction:**
    Museums are rapidly becoming vital components of the communities in which they are located. People congregate in these areas so that they can connect with one another, share ideas, and carry on conversations. It's not uncommon for museums to play host to community-building activities like meetings, performances, and other get-togethers. They have expanded beyond their usual

confines and now take an active part in talks taking place at the local and regional levels.
3. **Agents that Catalyze the Exchange of Cultures:**
Museums play an essential part in the process of fostering cultural interchange. They help tourists comprehend and appreciate the richness and diversity of human heritage while also facilitating discussion between different civilizations. Local audiences can see works of art, artifacts, and storytelling originating from all over the world thanks to the active participation of museums in international collaborations.
4. **Those Who Fight for Social Concerns:**

There has been a recent uptick in lobbying for a variety of social and political causes in museums. Through a variety of exhibitions, events, and activities, they tackle issues that are relevant to today's world, such as climate change, human rights, and social justice. Museums do more than merely monitor society; they also actively participate in changing the way people talk about society.

2. Recent Developments in Technological Fields

1. **Augmented Reality and Virtual Reality:**
The way that museums interact with visitors is being completely transformed by virtual and augmented reality. These technologies make it possible to have immersive experiences, which enable visitors to study ancient civilizations, move into historical circumstances, and see artworks come to life. The use of augmented reality apps and virtual tours can increase a visitor's level of engagement and comprehension.
2. **The Accessibility of Digital Collections:**
Museums are currently digitizing their collections in order to make them available to visitors all around the world. People are now able to view museum collections online, access educational resources, and do research from a remote location thanks to the advent of digital transformation. It makes museums much more accessible to more people and encourages inclusiveness.
3. **Interactive Displays and Various Forms of Media:**
Experiences that are engaging, informative, and interactive are becoming increasingly common in museums thanks to the proliferation of multimedia and interactive exhibitions. Touchscreen displays, interactive kiosks, and multimedia presentations provide visitors a more engaging and hands-on method of gaining knowledge.
4. **The Analyses of Data and the Personalization of Content:**
Data analytics is being used in museums to better understand the behavior and preferences of museum visitors. This strategy, which is driven by data, makes it possible for museums to personalize the experience of their visitors by giving

relevant material and recommendations. The level of engagement is increased by personalization, which also stimulates repeat visits.

5. **Participation in Online Communities and Use of Social Media:**

In order to interact with a more diverse demographic of people, museums are turning to online and social media channels. They engage in commercial, educational, and community-building activities on these platforms. Participation in online activities broadens the museum's presence beyond the confines of its physical location, thereby making it available to members of communities all over the world.

3. Being Inclusive and Respectful of Diversity

In the years to come, museums will place an even greater focus on welcoming people of all backgrounds. There has been a recent uptick in the number of efforts made by museums to guarantee that its collections, exhibitions, and staff members represent a diverse range of cultures, perspectives, and identities.

1. **The Process of Decolonization and Repatriation:**
   Museums all around the world are in the process of reassessing their collections and discussing topics of colonization as well as the purchase of cultural items. Recognizing the significance of ethical stewardship, a number of institutions are currently working for the return of objects to the nations in which they were first discovered.

2. **Engagement in the Community:**
   The practice of museums actively engaging with the communities that surround them, incorporating community members' voices and points of view into their exhibitions and programs, and involving them in the decision-making processes is becoming increasingly common.

3. **Multicultural and Diverse Representation:**
   It is important for museums to better reflect the communities they serve, hence efforts are being made to diversify museum staff, leadership, and governing bodies. Because of this diversity, decision-making and programming are able to benefit from a wider variety of perspectives.

4. **Confronting Preconceived Ideas:**

By providing depictions of civilizations, regions, and individuals that are more realistic and nuanced, museums are able to combat prejudices and misconceptions about those subjects. They encourage tourists to explore deeper beyond the surface stereotypes that they may have about the globe and embrace a more in-depth grasp of it.

4. Environmental Stewardship and the Maintenance of Sustainable Practices

The future of museums will feature an increased emphasis on environmentally responsible practices and sustainable practices. As people become more conscious of the effects of climate change and other environmental concerns, museums are becoming more committed to promoting sustainable practices and reducing their overall carbon footprint.

1. **Eco-Friendly Procedures at Museums:**
   The use of sustainable materials, decreased energy use, and waste prevention are some of the green practices that museums are implementing. These activities include recycling programs, energy-efficient lighting, and environmentally friendly building designs, among other things.
2. **Education Regarding Climate Change:**
   The platforms provided by many museums are being utilized to teach tourists about climate change and other environmental concerns. Museums promote a broader knowledge of the difficulties facing the world through a variety of means, including exhibitions, educational programs, and partnerships with environmental organizations.
3. **Ethical Sourcing: a Look at**
   The ethical origins of the materials and artifacts that make up a museum's collection are starting to receive increased attention from museum professionals. They are doing an investigation into the history of the objects and making certain that they were obtained in a moral and lawful manner.
4. **Methods of Transportation That Are Eco-Friendly:**

The mobility of artworks and artifacts is currently being investigated with a focus on eco-friendly transport alternatives by museums. This includes the use of packaging that is less harmful to the environment, modes of transportation that are less energy intensive, and less reliance on fossil fuels.

5. **Obstacles and Potential Breakthroughs**
The Obstacles:
Funding: Museums frequently run into financial difficulties, which can inhibit their capacity to innovate and extend their program offerings.

Accessibility: Ensuring that museums are accessible to all visitors, including those who have impairments, is a difficult task that calls for a commitment of both time and resources.

Digitization and Data Security While digitizing collections has many advantages, it also raises worries about data security, copyright issues, and the preservation of digital assets. While digitizing collections has many advantages, it also raises questions about data security.

Inclusion: A substantial amount of work and a continuing commitment are required in order to realize true inclusion and diversity within museums.

influence of Climate Change Museums are required to consider the influence that climate change will have on their collections, which may be susceptible to changes in the surrounding environment.

Occasions to seize:
Museums have the ability to partner with other institutions, such as libraries, archives, and universities, in order to pool resources and information for the purpose of doing research and developing programming that is more complete.

Virtual Participation Digital technology presents museums with new options to broaden their audience base, develop virtual exhibitions, and participate virtually with audiences all over the world.

Involvement of the Community Museums have the ability to involve local communities in both of the nations that are partners, which helps promote a sense of shared ownership and responsibility for cultural heritage.

Museums have the ability to contribute to a more sustainable future by implementing techniques known as sustainable practices. These activities can include energy-efficient operations and ecologically friendly exhibitions.

Connectivity on a Global Scale Because of advancements in technology and methods of communication, the globe is now more interconnected than ever before. This provides museums with the chance to attract visitors from all over the world and to promote greater intercultural understanding.

The future of museums is one that is dynamic and full of promise; it will be characterized by roles that are always shifting, technology advances, a focus on inclusivity, and a dedication to sustainability.

Museums will continue to play a crucial role in a variety of areas, including the promotion of intercultural understanding, the engagement of local communities, the dismantling of stereotypical beliefs, and the provision of platforms for educational and conversational exchange. Our society will continue to be enriched and more connected to the rest of the world thanks to the continued existence of key institutions like museums, which are always evolving to meet the new demands and opportunities of the 21st century.

9.1 Emerging trends and challenges

The 21st century has been a witness to a rapid alteration of our world in practically every area, ranging from technological advancements and commercial practices to political shifts and cultural shifts. As we make our way through this environment that is constantly shifting, we are forced to contend with developing patterns and obstacles that will have an impact on both our present and our future. In this essay, we will investigate some of the most major trends and issues that define the 21st century. These will range from technical breakthroughs and environmental concerns to geopolitical shifts and social dynamics. We will look at all of these topics and more.

1. **Developments in the Art of Technology**
1. **Robotics and Artificial Intelligence (also known as AI):**
   The use of AI and automation is causing a revolution in many different industries as well as the labor market. Although these technologies have the potential

to increase productivity, they also raise questions over the ethical use of AI and the displacement of jobs.
2. **IoT stands for the Internet of Things**
The Internet of Things (IoT) is a network that links commonly used items to the internet, which enables devices to exchange data and communicate with one another. This concept has applications in the healthcare industry as well as environmental monitoring and smart homes.
3. **The Technology of Blockchain:**
Blockchain is most well-known for its application in the realm of cryptocurrencies; however, it also has enormous potential applications in other fields, such as data security, supply chain management, and finance.
4. **Computing on the Quantum Level:**
The advent of quantum computing holds the promise of delivering an unprecedented level of processing power. This has repercussions for a variety of disciplines, including cryptography, materials science, and artificial intelligence, among others.
5. **Obstacles in the Field of Cybersecurity:**

The potential for harm from cyberattacks has grown along with the number of connected devices. The protection of sensitive data and vital infrastructure from attack by cybercriminals is a difficult and time-consuming task.

2. **Issues Related to the Environment**

1. **Environmental Degradation and the Impacts of Climate Change:**
The effects of climate change, which include a rise in average temperatures as well as an increase in the frequency and severity of extreme weather events, are becoming more and more apparent. Combating climate change is an issue that affects the entire world.
2. **Practices that are more sustainable and the use of renewable energy:**
The movement toward sustainable practices and renewable sources of energy is a trend that should be encouraged. Increasing the scope of these initiatives, however, in order to satisfy rising energy requirements, is a challenge.
3. **The Depletion of Biodiversity:**
The loss of biodiversity, which is caused by factors such as deforestation and the degradation of habitats, poses a threat to ecosystems and presents problems for conservation efforts.
4. **Lack of Access to Water:**

As a result of excessive consumption and pollution, many areas are experiencing water scarcity. It is of the utmost importance to guarantee that everyone has access to clean water.

3. Shifts in the Geopolitical Landscape

1. **The Ascendance of China:**
   A distinguishing trend is the rise of China's influence in both the political and economic spheres of the world. It brings into question the distribution of power and the dynamics of international relations.
2. **Concerns of a Global Nature:**
   Transcending national boundaries, issues such as terrorism, cyberwarfare, and pandemics present a challenge to conventional understandings of sovereignty and security.
3. **Movement of People and Forced Relocation:**

Both the nations that are the source of migrants and the countries that take them in face difficulties when dealing with mass migration because of variables such as war, the changing environment, and the economy.

4. The Nature of Social Change

1. **An Increasingly Older Population:**
   The elderly population presents a burden for a number of nations, which has repercussions for areas such as healthcare, pensions, and the labor market.
2. **The Rise of the City:**
   The number of people living in cities has increased to the point that they constitute the majority of the world's population. Challenges of essential importance include urban growth management and the resolution of difficulties related to housing, infrastructure, and transportation.
3. **The Diversity of Cultures:**
   The amount of cultural diversity is growing, which is making cultures more accepting of people of all backgrounds. However, it also presents difficulties in terms of intercultural understanding and the cohesiveness of the social fabric.
4. **The Role of Information and Social Media:**

Communication and the dissemination of ideas have been fundamentally altered as a result of the proliferation of social media and digital information. This gives rise to concerns over personal privacy, the spread of false information, and the power of social media platforms.

5. Concerning Health and Medical Care

1. **Contingency Planning for Pandemics:**
   The COVID-19 pandemic brought to light the importance of worldwide pandemic preparedness, highlighting the difficulties associated with the provision

of vaccines, the infrastructure of healthcare facilities, and international co-operation.
   2. **The Role of Technology in Healthcare and Telemedicine:**
   The rise in popularity of telemedicine and other forms of healthcare technology has opened up new avenues for the delivery of healthcare at a distance while simultaneously provoking new concerns over data access and protection.
   3. **Health of the Mind:**

As a result of increased knowledge and attempts to minimize stigma, mental health has received recognized as a key component of overall well-being. This is a positive development.

6. Changes in the Economic Climate

1. **Economy in the Digital Age:**
   E-commerce, remote employment, and digital currencies are some of the hallmarks of the quickly expanding digital economy, which calls for regulatory and taxation systems that can keep up with its rapid expansion.
2. **Unequal Distribution of Income:**
   The widening gap in incomes creates problems for social cohesiveness and for people's ability to take advantage of possibilities.
3. **International Distribution Networks:**

The COVID-19 pandemic brought to light vulnerabilities in global supply chains, which led to requests for supply networks that were both more resilient and varied.

7. Prioritizing Work and Education

1. **Work from home and other forms of flexible work arrangements:**
   The epidemic has hastened the adoption of remote work, which has sparked conversations about the future of work, the importance of maintaining a healthy work-life balance, and the availability of job prospects.
2. **Education Technology and Online Learning:**
   Learning that takes place online and the use of educational technology are causing a revolution in the educational system. While these developments improve accessibility and flexibility, they also raise concerns about the quality of education and the digital divide.
3. **Competencies and Recurrent Competencies:**

To remain competitive in today's rapidly evolving labor market, it is essential to continually update and broaden one's skill set.

8. Conundrums of a Moral and Ethical Nature

1. **Genetic Engineering and the Ethics of Biomedical Research:**
   New developments in genetic engineering, such as gene editing, pose difficult ethical questions because they involve the altering of living things.
2. **The Ethical Implications of Artificial Intelligence:**
   Ethical considerations in artificial intelligence, such as the potential for prejudice in algorithms and the effect on employment, are essential to the development of responsible AI.
3. **Issues of Confidentiality and Surveillance:**

In this day and age of digital technology, one of the most difficult challenges is maintaining a healthy balance between individual privacy and the need for security and monitoring.

The 21st century brings with it a wide variety of new tendencies and problems that will affect the world we live in. While advancements in technology present potential for innovation and growth, they also bring ethical and safety concerns that need to be addressed. Concerns about the environment bring to mind how critically important it is to implement sustainable policies. Alterations in geopolitical power dynamics call for innovative methods to diplomacy, while alterations in demographic makeup and cultural norms force our societies to adapt. Transformations in healthcare, education, and the workplace are occurring, and these changes have an effect on both markets and the distribution of income. It is vital for society to travel a route that embraces innovation, encourages inclusion, and solves critical global issues in order to establish a future that is better for everyone in spite of the trends and challenges that are currently present.

9.2 Sustainability and environmental responsibility in museums

Museums, in their capacity as keepers of cultural history and information, have an important part to play in the movement to promote sustainable practices and environmental stewardship. In recent years, there has been a rising realization within the community of museums of the need to embrace eco-friendly practices, decrease their carbon footprint, and contribute to the worldwide effort to conserve the environment. This has been one of the driving forces behind the Green Museum Initiative, which aims to make museums more environmentally responsible. Museums are expressing their dedication to conserving not only the past but also the future of our world through a combination of environmentally friendly operations and initiatives, educational outreach, and sustainable practices in museum operations.

1. **Methods That Are Environmentally Friendly**
   To lessen their negative effects on the surrounding environment, museums are increasingly implementing environmentally responsible business methods. This includes the installation of lighting systems that use less energy, the utilization of renewable energy sources such as solar power, and the optimization of heating,

ventilation, and air conditioning (HVAC) systems to reduce the amount of energy that is needed to run them. The installation of water-saving fixtures and water recycling systems are two of the primary strategies that many museums are employing in their efforts to reduce their overall water use.

In addition to that, environmentally responsible methods of waste management have emerged as a top issue for museums. In order to lessen the quantity of garbage that is produced, they are implementing recycling programs, cutting back on the usage of plastics that are only intended for one use, and encouraging composting. By putting an emphasis on environmentally friendly business practices, museums demonstrate to their local communities and the people who visit them the significance of environmentally conscious resource management.

2. **Ecologically Sound Projects**

Green programs that encourage people to be responsible for the environment and save it are increasingly being implemented in museums. Some organizations are adopting environmentally responsible building practices in both their new constructions and their renovations. These practices include the utilization of environmentally friendly materials and the addition of eco-friendly elements such as green roofs and rainwater collection systems. Museums are able to reduce their negative impact on the surrounding environment and provide an educational opportunity for visitors to learn about environmentally responsible construction when they adopt green building principles.

In addition, a growing number of museums are placing an emphasis on eco-friendly mobility choices for both their tourists and their employees. In order to promote environmentally friendly modes of mobility and cut down on carbon emissions, museums are doing things like encouraging visitors to take public transportation, establishing bike-sharing programs, and installing charging stations for electric vehicles, to name just a few examples.

3. **Outreach in the Field of Education**

The public is being educated about the importance of environmental preservation and sustainability by museums, which are capitalizing on the platforms they provide. They are doing this by holding seminars, educational programs, and interactive exhibitions about urgent environmental issues such as climate change, the loss of biodiversity, and the preservation of habitats. Museums are inspiring citizens to take action and make environmentally conscious decisions in their day-to-day lives by giving visitors with a deeper understanding of the significance of environmental stewardship and encouraging them to frequent the museums.

In addition, museums are working together with nearby schools and community organizations to establish educational programs that inspire the next generation of environmental advocates and foster environmental literacy. Museums are building a sustainable attitude among young learners by instilling in them a feeling of environmental responsibility. This, in turn, will help to the development of a society that is more ecologically conscious in the years to come.

4. Efforts should be Made in the Name of Conservation and Preservation

Museums are actively involved in conservation and preservation efforts to safeguard natural habitats and biodiversity, in addition to the work they make toward sustainable operations and educational outreach. The preservation of ecosystems, the protection of endangered species, and the funding of conservation projects are all being undertaken by a variety of organizations in partnership with environmental groups and academic institutions.

In addition, museums are making investments in the preservation of their own collections, establishing best practices for the preservation of artifacts, and making use of preservation procedures that are favorable to the environment. Museums are able to demonstrate their dedication to preserving the planet's biodiversity and fostering a sustainable future for all people by placing a higher priority on the conservation of natural history and cultural artifacts.

The principles of sustainability and environmental responsibility are increasingly being included into the overall aim of contemporary museums. Museums are leading by example in the fight to save the environment around the world by placing an emphasis on environmentally responsible business practices, launching environmentally conscious programs, participating in educational outreach, and making contributions to environmental protection efforts. Not only are museums working together to promote a more environmentally friendly future, but they are also encouraging visitors to take an active role in the drive toward environmental stewardship and conservation through the acts they do individually and collectively.

9.3 Museums and social justice

For a very long time, people have believed that museums are reservoirs of culture and history because they keep items and narratives from the past. However, just as the duties and responsibilities of museums change over time along with society, so too do museums themselves. In recent years, there has been a rising understanding of the potential for museums to serve as agents of social change, promoting social justice, equality, and inclusivity. This has led to an increase in the number of museums that seek to engage in these activities. In this essay, we will investigate how museums are transforming to embrace the ideas of social justice, including their efforts to challenge historical injustices, elevate the voices of those who are underrepresented, and connect with contemporary social challenges.

1. Bringing attention to historical wrongdoings

The questioning and remedying of historical wrongdoings are vital responsibilities that fall squarely on the shoulders of museums. Because they are frequently the

MUSEUMS AND GALLERIES

caretakers of the past, they have the ethical obligation to confront unsettling realities, acknowledge past wrongs, and work toward promoting reconciliation.

1. **The Process of Decolonization and Repatriation:**
   A great number of museums are in the process of critically examining their holdings and the part they play in the legacy of colonialism. Institutions are recognizing the ethical necessity of returning objects that were acquired through colonialism, theft, or other immoral ways, and as a result, they are working towards the repatriation of cultural artifacts to the nations in which they were originally discovered. This technique serves to correct historical wrongs and promotes reconciliation between museums and the communities that were negatively impacted by those wrongs.
2. **Discovering Long-Forgotten Histories:**

The goal of many museums nowadays is to unearth previously unknown historical facts that have been left out of more conventional accounts. They do research and outreach work in order to find and share the histories of underrepresented and underprivileged populations. By bringing to light history that had been ignored in the past, museums contribute to the process of restoring dignity and voice to individuals who have been historically marginalized.

2. **Giving a Voice to Those Who Are Underrepresented**

The mission of highlighting the voices of individuals who have been excluded from or underrepresented in traditional narratives is becoming increasingly important to museums. This entails actively searching out various points of view and aggressively incorporating them into their collections and shows.

1. **More Inclusive Methods of Curatorial Work:**
   In order to ensure that a wider variety of perspectives are taken into consideration during the decision-making process, museums are broadening the curatorial teams and leadership roles within their institutions. Because of this diversity, the curation may be made to be more inclusive and representative.
2. **Engagement in the Community:**
   A growing number of museums are inviting members of the communities surrounding them to participate in the curatorial process. They want to make sure that the exhibitions and programs they put on represent the concerns and ambitions of the communities that they serve, therefore they solicit input and collaboration from the community.
3. **The Presentation of Material in Collections:**

Artworks, antiques, and historical things that are representative of the breadth of the human experience are increasingly being collected by museums and displayed in these establishments. This includes gathering and exhibiting works produced by artists and producers hailing from a variety of backgrounds, with the goal of providing narratives that are more inclusive.

3. Addressing the Emerging Social Problems of Today

Museums are doing more than just preserving the past; they are also actively engaged with the social challenges of the present and the future. Exhibits, projects, and initiatives are being developed by museums that confront contemporary concerns, advocate for social justice, and inspire discussion and contemplation.

1. **Displays Concerning Social Justice:**
   Exhibitions that investigate topics concerning social justice are frequently staged in museums. Topics that are frequently investigated include racial injustice, gender discrimination, environmental justice, and human rights. These exhibitions serve as a forum for discussion and bring attention to the issues that are of the utmost importance.
2. **Collaborative Efforts and Strategic Alliances:**
   In order to address the modern societal challenges of our time, museums are forming partnerships with local community organizations, advocacy groups, and activists. Through these kind of partnerships, museums are able to contribute to continuing initiatives for social justice and help create change.
3. **Educational Programs and Activities:**

The development of educational programs and resources that educate the general public on matters pertaining to social justice constitutes an important part of the mission of most museums, which is to play an active role in promoting greater levels of awareness and education. These activities provide individuals with knowledge, which in turn encourages empathy and an awareness of others' perspectives.

4. Access and Representation That Are Open to All

Museums are making efforts to ensure that their facilities and resources are open to and welcoming of a wide variety of visitors by implementing the appropriate measures. This includes taking steps to make museums physically accessible to those who have disabilities, providing interpretative materials in many languages or that are relevant to a particular culture, and making accommodations for a variety of learning methods.

1. **Providing Access to Everyone:**
   Visitors with disabilities are the focus of efforts being made by museums to improve access to both their buildings and displays. This includes the provision of ramps, elevators, tactile guides, interpreters of sign language, and any other adjustments that may be necessary.
2. **Interpretation That Takes Into Account Multiple Languages And Cultures:**
   Interpretive materials are being made available in a variety of languages, and

museums are beginning to incorporate culturally relevant storytelling. Because of this, exhibitions and collections are accessible to a wider demographic of people.

3. **Accessibility in the Digital and Online World:**

Museums are also addressing digital accessibility, which involves ensuring that online displays and resources are accessible to those who may not be able to physically visit the museum as well as people who have disabilities that prevent them from doing so.

Both difficulties and prospects are involved.

It is possible for some institutions to be resistant to change and to continue to be bound to their conventional narratives and practices.

limits on Resources: Museums sometimes contend with resource limits, particularly financial ones, which can hinder their capacity to apply inclusive policies or establish new programs.

Expectations of Visitors Museums have a difficult task ahead of them as they strive to evolve toward social justice aims while also meeting the expectations of their regular visitors.

On the other hand, there are a number of big opportunities:

Support from the Public: Numerous tourists and local populations are in favor of the transformation of museums into agents of social justice.

Collaboration: Efforts made by museums, communities, and organizations to work together toward a common goal can have a greater overall impact on the fight for social justice.

Participation in Digital Activities: Participation in digital activities provides museums with new chances to reach a worldwide audience and participate in discourses about social justice.

Museums are changing to embrace their roles as agents of social justice by addressing modern social challenges, exposing historical injustices, and elevating perspectives that have been underrepresented. By doing so, they not only fulfill their duty to preserving the past but also play an active role in crafting a future that is more equal and inclusive. This is because they have fulfilled their commitment to preserve the past. Museums have the capacity to act as catalysts for change by promoting a society that values social justice and the dignity of all of its members. This can be accomplished by encouraging dialogue, understanding, and empathy among museum visitors.

9.4 Speculations on the future of museums

As cultural institutions, museums have always been able to adjust to the shifting requirements and standards of the society they serve. They are up against a plethora of difficulties and opportunities in the 21st century, all of which will continue to have an impact on their future. This essay will investigate many hypotheses on the future of museums, focusing on how these establishments are likely to develop in response to emerging technologies, altering demographics, growing concerns regarding the environment, and evolving cultural dynamics.

1. **Developments in technology and the transition**
1. **Virtual Reality (VR) and Augmented Reality (AR):**
   Virtual reality (VR) and augmented reality (AR) have the potential to completely change the way visitors experience museums. Visitors will be able to experience immersive exhibitions from the convenience of their own homes, step into historical locations, and interact with digital reconstructions of items. Visitors will also have the option to step into historical settings. Through the use of virtual reality, people from all over the world might "visit" museums without ever having to leave the comfort of their own homes, hence increasing participation and accessibility.
2. **Electronic Archives and Collections:**
   The process of digitizing museum collections to make them available to a wider audience across the world is gaining momentum. Visitors will be able to virtually explore collections through the use of online platforms, which will include high-resolution photographs, comprehensive information, and interactive elements. This digital accessibility will not take the place of actual visits; rather, it will supplement those visits by giving additional context and information.
3. **Personalization Based On The Analysis Of Data:**
   Data analytics will be used in museums to personalize the experience of their guests. By monitoring the preferences and actions of visitors, museums are able to deliver individualized recommendations, guided tours, and interactive components that are tailored to the visitors' specific areas of interest. This level of customization boosts engagement among visitors and motivates them to come back again.
4. **Participation in Digital Activities:**

Museums will engage with audiences through the use of social media, mobile applications, and digital platforms in order to cultivate an online community that is interested in their collections and programming on a worldwide scale. The museum's presence will be extended beyond its physical location through the use of online engagement, which will enable the museum to reach a target audience that is both more numerous and more varied.

2. **Changes in the Demographic Makeup and Inclusivity**

1. **An Increasingly Older Population:**
   The needs and interests of elderly visitors will need to be taken into consideration by museums as populations continue to age. There will be an increase in

the number of exhibitions and events that are centered on issues such as health, wellness, and preparation for retirement.
2. **The Diversity of Cultures:**
As the number of people from different cultural backgrounds grows, museums will strive to become more inclusive and representative. They will make it a top priority to acquire artworks, objects, and tales that reflect a more diverse variety of cultures and points of view, and they will show these items prominently.
3. **Accessibility for People of Multiple Languages and Cultures:**

Interpretive materials will be made available in a variety of languages, and culturally relevant displays will be presented in museums so as to cater to a wide range of visitors. Because of this, museum spaces and resources will be more welcoming to people from all over the world.

3. A Responsible Approach to the Environment and Long-Term Sustainability

1. **Environmentally Friendly Programs:**
Many museums are already implementing environmentally friendly policies and procedures, such as lighting that uses less energy and sustainable architectural designs.
It is possible that in the future, museums may rely more on renewable energy sources, add green roofs, and promote environmentally friendly operations in order to reduce their impact on the surrounding environment.
2. **Education Regarding Climate Change:**

There will be a shift toward museums playing a more major role in educating tourists about climate change and other environmental concerns. Through the use of exhibitions, activities, and partnerships with environmental organizations, a better awareness of the difficulties that our planet faces will be promoted.

4. Participation in Community Life and Co-Creation

1. **Partnerships with the Community:**
In order to design programs that are reflective of the concerns and ambitions of the local community, museums will collaborate with nearby schools, community organizations, and advocacy groups. Input from the local community will play an increasingly important part in the development of exhibitions and programming.
2. **Exhibitions That Are Co-Curated:**

Community members will be invited to participate in the curating process at museums, and they will be given the opportunity to co-create exhibitions that are reflective of their own experiences and points of view. Taking this strategy will result in exhibitions that are both more relevant and more authentic.

5. Issues of Social Justice and Other Modern Concerns

1. **Initiatives Regarding Social Justice:**
   Museums will continue to confront modern concerns such as racial injustice, gender discrimination, and human rights through the use of exhibitions, programming, and advocacy initiatives in the future. The pursuit of social justice will continue to be a priority for a great number of organizations.
2. **Efforts Made in Collaboration:**

In order to address urgent societal problems, museums will work together with local community organizations, advocacy groups, and individual activists. Because of these connections, museums will be able to take a more active role in the fight for social justice and equity.

6. Accessibility and hybridization of experiences

1. **Hybrid Exhibitions:**
   The public will be able to explore museum exhibits in both the conventional and digital formats through the creation of new exhibitions that combine digital and physical components by museums.
2. **Providing Access to Everyone:**

The accessibility of museums will be given a higher priority, and museum staff will make every effort to ensure that their physical locations and online resources are accessible to visitors with disabilities. They are going to utilize technology in order to provide accessible tours, interpretation in sign language, and tactile guidance.

Both difficulties and prospects are involved

The Obstacles:

limits on Resources: Museums frequently suffer resource limits, such as limited financial resources, which might hinder their ability to embrace inclusive policies and new technologies.

Expectations of Visitors: In order to meet the expectations of traditional visitors, who value the

analog, tactile, and in-person features of museum visits, museums need to strike a balance between developing for the future and advancing toward the present.

There are some institutions that may be resistant to change and continue to be wedded to established narratives and practices, which will slow down the institution's ability to adapt to the changing world.

Occasions to seize:

Support from the Public A significant number of tourists and communities are on board with the movement of museums toward a future that is more welcoming, technologically advanced, and socially engaged.

Collaboration: Efforts made together by communities, organizations, and museums have the potential to have a greater impact in the areas of social justice, sustainability, and inclusivity.

Participation in Digital Activities: Participation in digital activities provide museums with new chances to reach audiences all over the world and to participate in conversations about important social and environmental concerns.

The future of museums is fraught with both fascinating opportunities and difficult obstacles to overcome. Museums will play an increasingly important role in fostering debate, understanding, and change as technology continues to improve, demographics continue to move, and global concerns continue to become more urgent. They need to be able to adapt to new circumstances and be willing to accept a future that embraces inclusion, engages with contemporary issues, and makes use of technology to increase their reach while still maintaining their crucial position as guardians of culture and history. This will be the key to their success.

www.ingramcontent.com/pod-product-compliance
Lightning Source LLC
LaVergne TN
LVHW021047100526
838202LV00079B/4723